Praise for *California Dreaming*

"Mayors, governors, and other policymakers around the country are struggling to maintain services while paying for the skyrocketing costs of public employee retirement benefits. *California Dreaming* explains why it is so difficult to solve this problem and identifies a key framework for solutions."

> —**Chuck Reed**, former Mayor, City of San Jose, California

"*California Dreaming* is as important as an early warning of an impending tsunami. Ignoring its message would be equally irresponsible. Underfunding fixed pension benefits for California employees with an inadequate portfolio of risky assets will eventually fail catastrophically. Almost everyone, particularly future taxpayers, will suffer. As with a tsunami warning, quick action offers the opportunity of minimizing the damage from current policies. Lawrence McQuillan offers a thoughtful menu of policy reforms which would improve the situation dramatically."

> —**John B. Shoven**, Charles R. Schwab Professor of Economics and Trione Director of the Stanford Institute of Economic Policy Research, Stanford University

"Unfunded public pensions and healthcare are the greatest threats to government financial stability in our country. Over 80% of the government bodies in California are headed for bankruptcy for owing more than a half trillion dollars in unfunded pension and healthcare debt. Mounting debt will force the closing of public libraries, parks, and schools. Police and fire services will be cut, streets will be in disrepair, and we will find ourselves living in a Third World country. Lawrence McQuillan's outstanding book *California Dreaming* spells out these disasters about to happen with perfect clarity."

> —**Richard J. Riordan**, former Mayor, City of Los Angeles, California

"Public employee pensions could be the next fiscal crisis—trillions of dollars placed in increasingly risky investments, managed by organizations with little understanding of the risks, operating under accounting rules that provide little transparency for elected officials and citizens to understand what is going on. Lawrence J. McQuillan's important book *California Dreaming* shows how the Golden State's pension system encouraged policymakers to promise too much, fund too little, and take excessive risk with the plan's investments. But McQuillan does not merely have lessons for Californians. Citizens across the country need to learn more about the risk posed by public pensions and how to fix those plans, and *California Dreaming* is a great place to start."

> —**Andrew G. Biggs**, Resident Scholar, American Enterprise Institute

"*California Dreaming* is a horrifying must read that exposes the steal-as-you-go policy driving the state straight down the tubes!"

> —**Laurence J. Kotlikoff**, William Fairfield Warren Distinguished Professor and Professor of Economics, Boston University; former Senior Economist, President's Council of Economic Advisers

"Governments have a tendency to commit to tasks that they really cannot deliver on. Public pensions are an example of this general tendency. Generous promises are made and then underfunded because of the pressures of elective office. *California Dreaming* provides very useful evidence of both the generosity of the unsustainable promises made to California's public-sector employees, and the failure to fully pay for those promises. The result may be a fiscal catastrophe for Californian taxpayers and retirees in the not-too-distant future—unless this very timely book's reforms are adopted in the next few years."

> —**Roger D. Congleton**, BB&T Professor of Economics, West Virginia University

"California, the canary in the coalmine for practically all of America's states, faces an enormous and largely unacknowledged crisis in its system of pensions for teachers and other public employees. In *California Dreaming*, Lawrence J. McQuillan writes that those pensions 'are like tapeworms in the guts of public treasuries.' The result is a shortfall of more than half a trillion dollars. The good news, though, is that McQuillan has the answer—a handful of reforms to fix California's pension problem permanently, and a lesson for the rest of the states in this very important, timely, and well-researched book."

> —**James K. Glassman**, Visiting Fellow, American Enterprise Institute; Member, SEC Investor Advisory Committee; former U.S. Under Secretary of State for Public Diplomacy; former Publisher, *The New Republic*; former President, *The Atlantic Monthly*

"Lawrence McQuillan's *California Dreaming* is a superb, wake-up call to all those depending on generous pensions from state and local governments—they simply won't be there, or at least in the amounts expected. The book is also a wake-up call to California taxpayers—who will be shocked to learn of the huge tax liabilities they face. McQuillan explains how governments have created this mess and offers sensible reforms to end the crisis and preserve retirement benefits—without bankrupting taxpayers."

> —**James C. Miller III**, former Director, U.S. Office of Management and Budget; former Chairman, Federal Trade Commission; former Executive Director, Presidential Task Force on Regulatory Relief

"Politicians must learn not to make retirement finding decisions for city and state employees and not be able to fulfill them. It is unfair to current and future employees as well as the general public to carry the financial burden of past, unrealistic, unfunded liabilities. *California Dreaming* is the right book at the perfect time to explain the issues and suggest a realistic approach. The public needs to hold politicians much more accountable or suffer the financial consequences."

—**Frank M. Jordan**, former Mayor and former Chief of Police,
City and County of San Francisco, California

"California's policymakers are living in Fantasy Land, as they downplay the depth of the state's pension crisis. In *California Dreaming*, Lawrence McQuillan does a remarkable service explaining why the public pension systems are broken. He then offers sensible solutions for fixing them, and all California officials should listen. This is a great book for anyone who wants to understand an issue that unless averted will erode public services, destroy budgets and bankrupt our future."

—**Steven M. Greenhut**, columnist, *U-T San Diego*

"In *California Dreaming*, Lawrence McQuillan does a great job of clearly explaining how the mismanagement of California's state pension plans has led to massive unfunded pension liabilities. McQuillan offers sensible policy reforms to address California's pension crisis, and explains why all Californians would benefit from those reforms. Unfunded pension liabilities plague many states, and this book offers the clearest explanation on how the problem arises and how it can best be addressed."

—**Randall G. Holcombe**, DeVoe Moore Professor of Economics,
Florida State University

"The message of this highly readable volume is both realistic and hopeful: The California public pension system is an economic time bomb, yet the explosion is not inevitable. Lawrence McQuillan points the way to six reforms that would not only defuse California's problems but would also benefit other states in the same predicament. I recommend *California Dreaming* to anyone who wants to understand the scope of the public pension crisis, how we got there, and what we can do to effect a permanent solution."

—**William E. Simon, Jr.**, Co-Chairman, William E. Simon & Sons, LLC; former Candidate for Governor of California; former Assistant U.S. Attorney for the Southern District of New York

California
Dreaming

California
Dreaming
Lessons on How to Resolve America's Public Pension Crisis

LAWRENCE J. MCQUILLAN

INDEPENDENT
INSTITUTE
Oakland, California

Independent Institute
100 Swan Way, Oakland, CA 94621-1428
Telephone: 510-632-1366
Fax: 510-568-6040
Email: info@independent.org
Website: www.independent.org

Cover design: Denise Tsui
Cover image: Alloy Photography / Veer

Library of Congress Cataloging-in-Publication Data

McQuillan, Lawrence J., 1961–
    California dreaming: lessons on how to resolve America's public pension crisis / Lawrence J. McQuillan.
        pages cm
    ISBN 978-1-59813-243-4 (hardcover : alk. paper) 978-1-59813-189-5 (pbk. : alk. paper)
1. California—Officials and employees—Pensions. 2. Pensions—Government policy—California. I. Title.
    JK8760.P4M37 2015
    331.25'291351794—dc23   2014048961

To my family—
Marian, Kathleen, Rob, Teddy, and Charm—
whose love and support have helped to
sustain me and my work

Contents

Tables and Figures

Tables

Figures

Acknowledgements

A PROJECT OF this magnitude is never completely the work of the author. Many others made important contributions and suggestions that improved the book.

First, I thank the peer reviewers who provided more than a half-dozen detailed reviews with ideas, insights, questions, and comments that helped refine the arguments and policy recommendations. Their decades of experience in economics, law, and public service were invaluable in providing constructive feedback.

Special thanks to Adriana N. Vazquez, a graduate in economics from the University of California, Berkeley, and policy research assistant at the Independent Institute, for providing outstanding research support and help constructing the graphics. I also relied on the world-class libraries at U.C. Berkeley for some research materials. Intern Shelby S. Sullivan also provided editorial assistance for which I am grateful.

I thank several staff members of the California legislature and state pension funds for answering my questions regarding California public pension operations and legislation.

I and almost everyone in the country who is interested in public pension issues, rely on the web site PensionTsunami.com, published by Jack Dean, to stay current on pension developments in California and across the country. I don't know how Jack does it, but he provides a comprehensive and valuable service for everyone interested in pension news and pension policy.

I also thank everyone who attended my discussions on an earlier draft of the book at the Economic Roundtable of San Francisco, the Old Capital Club in Monterey, California, and the Infinity Towers in San Francisco. The talks and accompanying Q and A's helped clarify points and ultimately improved the final version of the book.

Special thanks to Norman J. Laboe who provided financial support for the book, and to Donald H. Korn who spent many hours with me discussing pension issues based on his decades of experience in financial analysis.

Finally, I am indebted to the staff of the Independent Institute: Roy M. Carlisle for shepherding the book through the production process; Gail Saari and Dawn Adams for production management and copyediting, respectively; Denise Tsui for the cover, Leigh McLellan for the layout; and David Theroux, Mary Theroux, and Martin Buerger for entrusting me with this important project.

This book was born from a love of California and a recognition that if it is to remain a place where our children and grandchildren can pursue their dreams and passions, then our generation must solve the greatest financial challenge facing the Golden State—its crushing public pension costs.

My views and conclusions in the book do not necessarily represent those of the board, supporters, or staff of the Independent Institute.

Lawrence J. McQuillan, PhD
Director, Center on Entrepreneurial Innovation
Independent Institute
Oakland, California

Introduction

AS THE WORLD'S eighth-largest economy, California is a prosperous state. In 2013, the Golden State produced $2.2 trillion of goods and services—more than India and about 12 percent of the U.S. total.[1] There are many reasons for the state's prosperity, beginning with its weather.

The "California lifestyle" of sun, surf, and endless summers has acted as a magnet for people living in the Snow Belt and from around the world.[2] California is now the nation's most populous state with 38.5 million people, more than 12 percent of the U.S. population.[3]

California also is home to many of the world's finest universities, Silicon Valley, and top aerospace and biotech companies. The fabric of California is woven with threads of entrepreneurship, innovation, and risk-taking,

---

1. See California Department of Finance, Financial and Economic Data, "California State Gross Domestic Product, 1963 through 2012," accessed April 2, 2014; U.S. Department of Commerce, Bureau of Economic Analysis, "Gross Domestic Product," accessed April 2, 2014; The World Bank, "GDP," accessed April 2, 2014.

2. California has the twelfth highest average annual temperature, and it is the sixth best state for average annual sunshine. See Current Results, "Average Annual Temperature for Each U.S. State," and "Average Annual Sunshine by State," accessed September 11, 2014. California also has the second-longest saltwater coastline in the lower forty-eight states—second to Florida.

3. U.S. Department of Commerce, Census Bureau, "State and County QuickFacts," accessed April 2, 2014.

producing the country's third most diversified economy.[4] And all of these new products can reach the world from California.

California has a vast network of deep-water ports and interstate highways that link the state to trading partners in the United States and around the world, especially in Canada, Mexico, Asia, and South America.[5]

Warm, sunny weather, combined with rising income and an innovative economy have attracted people to the Golden State, producing big exciting cities. Yet in this land of plenty, decay and decline are visible everywhere.

Public libraries, parks, and recreation facilities are shortening their hours or closing. Potholes go unfilled, sidewalks unrepaired, and trees untrimmed. California has the nation's fourth-worst highway system, with crumbling roads, bridges, and tunnels.[6]

Police refuse to respond to a growing list of crimes in some of the state's largest cities. Response times are lengthening for police, fire, and emergency medical technicians (EMTs), with fewer police officers and firefighters to respond to more calls for service. And money for classroom instruction has been disappearing. What explains this contradiction in the land of plenty?

In large part the cause is California's unaffordable pensions for government employees, which are consuming ever-larger shares of government budgets at the state and local levels. Public pensions are like tapeworms in the guts of public treasuries, starving governments of money needed to fund traditional

---

4. John E. Wagner and Steven C. Deller, "Measuring the Effects of Economic Diversity on Growth and Stability," *Land Economics* 74, no. 4 (November 1998), 541–56.

5. Measured by tons of cargo, California has four of the nation's top forty ports: Long Beach (fifth in the United States), Los Angeles (ninth), Richmond (twenty-ninth), and Oakland (thirty-fifth). See American Association of Port Authorities, U.S. Port Ranking by Cargo Volume 2010. California ports are the nearest coastal port for shippers as far away as parts of New Mexico and Colorado. See Jordan Rappaport and Jeffrey D. Sachs, "The United States as a Coastal Nation," *Journal of Economic Growth* 8, no. 1 (March 2003), 5–46.

6. David T. Hartgen, M. Gregory Fields, and Elizabeth San Jose, *20th Annual Report on the Performance of State Highway Systems*, Policy Study 406 (Los Angeles: Reason Foundation, July 2013).

public services that our parents and grandparents once enjoyed and robbing future generations of the California dream.

Unlike most retirement plans offered by private companies, government workers receive defined-benefit pensions that guarantee specific monthly payments to retirees for life, regardless of how well the pension-fund investments perform. This puts taxpayers on the hook to make up any difference between pension promises and pension assets.

As we will see, rising pension costs, fueled by the deceptions and mismanagement of public officials, have caused several California cities to declare bankruptcy. Other California communities are considering joining them.

Meanwhile, the massive tax increases needed to make state and local pension funds solvent have proven to be politically impossible to enact, making the pension systems financially unsustainable. The failure to fully fund the pension promises has allowed the current generation to receive public services that they are not fully paying for, pushing the pension problem onto future generations. This is a classic form of deficit spending, but not constrained by state balanced budget requirements. Politicians kick the can down the road as pension debts mount.

The unwillingness to confront the true scope of California's pension costs, to pay for the promises made, and to make changes to control future obligations means these costs are being pushed onto our children and grandchildren, who are being forced to pay for promises they did not make and for services they did not agree to. The injustice of this system is apparent to anyone who cares to see.

This "big mess," as Governor Jerry Brown once described it,[7] has grown to unsustainable levels. Left unchanged, the financial burden of public pensions will crush our children and grandchildren, leaving them with a depleted future and a depleted California. The responsibility to fix this problem is as

---

7. *Governor Brown Announces Pension Reform Agreement to Save Billions by Capping Benefits, Increasing the Retirement Age, and Stopping Abuse*, press release, August 28, 2012.

great as any moral imperative because it directly impacts the quality of life our children will enjoy and their chances for upward mobility. California's public pension crisis is the state's greatest financial challenge since the Great Depression. And anyone who thinks the current public pension structure in California is sustainable is dreaming.

This book explains how California got into its pension mess, how big the problem is, and why it has not been fixed. It shows that pension officials and politicians of both political parties deliberately low-balled the contributions, increased the benefits, and underfunded pensions on a massive scale. True unfunded liabilities are up to nearly four times larger than official government estimates: nearly $15,000 per Californian. It is unrealistic to believe that California will tax or invest its way out of this problem. Changes must be made.

This book provides a blueprint for how to fix California's public pension problems in an equitable, responsible, and moral way that preserves pension benefits already earned, provides competitive pensions going forward, and grants the flexibility needed so that future generations are not paying for deals they did not make and can receive all of the traditional public services they desire in the future.

Current and future retirees would be wise to accept the recommended reforms because the alternative could be much worse for them, as Detroit foreshadows. Detroit, which filed for Chapter 9 federal bankruptcy protection in July 2013 primarily because of unaffordable public pensions, exited bankruptcy in December 2014 under an agreement to reduce the pension checks of current and future city retirees. Public pensions are no longer untouchable.

Most of the policy recommendations presented here are already in place in the private sector. Many academics and professional associations in economics, finance, and actuarial science support them. The changes would bring public-sector pensions in line with those in the private sector and would ensure that California never confronts this crisis again.

The dream is to resolve the pension crisis equitably and permanently so California governments are not deadbeat institutions—skipping out on financial obligations to push them onto our kids. The reforms would fix the Golden State's pension problems, helping to restore the California dream.

California is not the only state with massive public pension debt and pension costs that are devouring government services. Similar crises exist in Connecticut, Florida, Illinois, New Jersey, New York, Ohio, Pennsylvania, and West Virginia, to name a few. And cities, such as Chicago, Los Angeles, New York, and Philadelphia, face their own local pension crises. This book provides a blueprint for America on how to measure the true extent of a pension problem, identify the political drivers of a crisis, and make strong fiscal and moral arguments in favor of pension reforms that would permanently fix the problem. The book provides methods and hard lessons learned in California that can be applied anywhere in America.

SECTION I

The Problems

SECTION I PRESENTS essential information on the operation of California's public pension systems and how they have gotten into such severe financial problems. Chapter 1 looks at the structure of California's public pension systems and explains how defined-benefit pensions are calculated. Chapter 2 explains how pension funds are amassed.

Chapter 3 presents various measures of the health of the state's defined benefit government pension systems. It explains why official measures of funding status are seriously flawed, and that correct measurements reveal California's public pension systems are much more unhealthy than officially reported. Chapter 4 answers the question: How did we get to where we are? It highlights the critical actions that drove California's public pension debt sky-high. Most of the actions were self-inflicted—related to poor public governance, not macroeconomic developments.

Chapter 5 examines the perverse incentives facing lawmakers and pension officials that cause them to mismanage public pensions and allow the problems to escalate. Finally, Chapter 6 discusses the immorality of pushing

1

pension costs onto future generations. Our children and grandchildren receive few benefits, if any, from past government spending, and while not consenting to the spending or pension amounts, they will have to pay for the pension costs through higher taxes, reduced services, or a combination of both. The analysis used, and the lessons learned, can be applied to any state or municipality in America struggling with its own public pension problem.

1

How Are Defined-Benefit Pensions Calculated?

THE VAST MAJORITY of California's public pension systems operate as defined-benefit (DB) plans, meaning that these plans pay a specific pension amount to their retirees each month for life. In total, about 4 million Californians—11 percent of the population—are members of one or more of the state's 86 defined-benefit public pension systems: 6 state plans, 21 county plans, 32 city plans, and 27 special district and other plans.[1,2]

Some plans are small and run by a single city or county. Other plans are huge statewide systems. The "Big Three" are the California Public Employees' Retirement System (CalPERS), the California State Teachers' Retirement System (CalSTRS), and the University of California Retirement Plan (UCRP). CalPERS and CalSTRS are the largest and second-largest public pension systems in the country, respectively.

CalPERS is a pension system for 1.68 million current and former state and local government employees and their families (see Figure 1.1). More than 3,000 public-sector employers participate in CalPERS (1,581 public agencies at the city, county, or state level and 1,508 school districts covering the nonteaching employees, such as janitors and office workers). Employees with

---

1. John Chiang, *Public Retirement Systems Annual Report* (Sacramento: California State Controller Office, May 2013), i–iv.

2. All of the numbers in the book were current as of the date the book went to typesetting. Keep in mind, however, that the numbers can change over time, especially the numbers provided by the public pension funds themselves. Please use the sources cited to find updated editions and more current numbers, if necessary and if available.

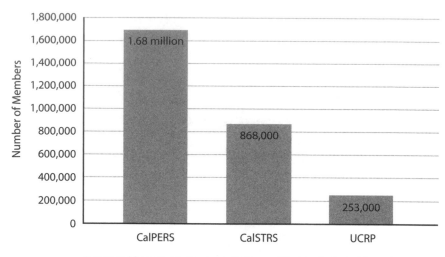

Sources: California Public Employees' Retirement System, *Facts at a Glance*, January 2014; California State Teachers' Retirement System, *Fast Facts*, accessed January 28, 2014; and University of California, *Retirement System 2013–2014 Annual Financial Report* (Oakland: University of California Office of the President, November 5, 2014), 4.

Figure 1.1. Membership in California's three largest state-operated public pension funds

the twenty-three campus California State University system are members of CalPERS.

CalSTRS serves 868,000 current and retired K–12 and community college public school teachers and their families. About 1,600 employers (school districts, community college districts, and county offices of education) participate.

UCRP serves 253,000 active, inactive, and retired employees of the University of California system and their families. Participating employers include the university's ten campuses, five medical centers, Lawrence Berkeley National Laboratory, and Hastings College of the Law.

Cities and counties have the option of participating in CalPERS and/or CalSTRS, or they can create their own independent pension system.

DB payments for retirees are calculated based on (1) the number of years of service; (2) age at retirement; and (3) final compensation, which is typically the highest annual pay plus special compensation averaged over a 3-year period.

There are variations, however, in the number of years used to calculate "final compensation." Some California teachers with 25 years or more of service, for example, can use their highest consecutive 12-month period of pay to calculate final compensation. Making the pension calculations more complicated, a variety of formulas are applied depending on the employer (state, school, or local government agency), occupation (general office, safety, industrial, or police/fire), and the specific terms in the contract between the employer (government agency) and the pension fund.

To illustrate how a pension benefit is calculated, a state employee hired under CalPERS's "2 percent at 55" can retire at age 55 with 2 percent of their final compensation for every year they have worked.[3] If an employee with 30 years on the job, having earned a final compensation of $100,000 a year,[4] chooses to retire at age 55, then that employee will receive 60 percent (30 × 2 percent) of his or her compensation, or $60,000 annually for life.

If this same employee retires at age 63 or older, the "benefit factor" rises from 2 percent to 2.5 percent, meaning that after 30 years on the job, he or she would receive 75 percent (30 × 2.5 percent) of compensation, or $75,000 annually for life. Note that DB "benefit factors" are back loaded, meaning they increase with age and, therefore, reward additional service years at an increasing rate.

Pension calculation formulas can also vary with occupation. For example, some local police officers and firefighters can retire through CalPERS at age 50 with 3 percent of final compensation for every year served. And pension calculation formulas can vary by jurisdiction. For example, Orange County's pension system permits a 2.7 percent benefit factor at age 55 for some

---

3. See CalPERS's retirement benefit formula charts here.

4. CalPERS members who enrolled on or after January 1, 2013, have caps on the amount of compensation used to calculate their benefit of either $115,064 (members coordinated with Social Security) or $138,077 (members not coordinated with Social Security) in 2014. The cap is adjusted annually based on the Consumer Price Index for all Urban Consumers. See California Public Employees' Retirement System, *Your CalPERS Benefits: Planning Your Service Retirement* (Sacramento: CalPERS, 2013), 6.

PENSION SPIKING

Most public-sector collective bargaining agreements include automatic annual cost-of-living adjustments (COLAs) or automatic "step increases" for length of time on the job, or both. These features automatically increase base pay used to ultimately calculate pension benefits, and neither is typically available in the private sector. Pension payments to retirees are often increased annually through automatic COLAs as well.

The "special compensation" used to calculate pensions includes overtime pay, unused vacation pay, allowances, and bonuses. To the extent possible, each employee has a strong incentive to bump these up in the last few years of service since these are the years used to calculate pension benefits. This practice is called *pension spiking*. The fewer the number of years that are used to calculate final compensation the more attractive pension spiking becomes to workers.

Under current federal law, a private-sector pension cannot be based on an average compensation using fewer than 5 years. State and local pensions are exempt from this law; thus, public pensions in California typically use 3 years or less of earnings to calculate pension benefits, making spiking very attractive and beneficial. Very few state workers

non-public-safety workers. The largest group of state workers is under a "2 at 55" formula with CalPERS.[5]

The California Rule

California's defined-benefit public pensions pay a specified amount to each retiree for life. In what has come to be called the *California Rule*, public-

---

5. Jon Ortiz, "The Public Eye: California Public Pension Payouts Doubled After Bump in Benefits," *Sacramento Bee*, September 9, 2013.

have yet to retire under an "average-of-three-years" formula—most are less than three years.

Through spiking, lifetime annual pensions for some retired government workers exceed their final year's pay. For example, retired Ventura County Sheriff Bob Brooks receives an annual pension of $283,000.[1] His final salary was $227,600. Former Merced County Sheriff Mark Pazin receives a higher annual pension than he received in pay when working—nearly $200,000 a year.[2] Former San Francisco Police Chief Heather Fong was paid more than $528,000 in her last year as chief, but more than $303,000 of that were payouts for unused sick, vacation, and comp time before retirement. Fong, who left office at age 53, receives a public pension of $277,656 a year for life, a lot more money than she received when working ($187,875).[3]

---

1. Ed Mendel, "Ventura County Pension Reform Has Poster Child," *Cal-Pensions*, January 27, 2014.

2. Ramona Giwargis, "Former Sheriff Mark Pazin's Pension from Merced County Nears $200,000," *Merced Sun-Star*, February 17, 2014.

3. Phillip Matier and Andrew Ross, "Retiring S.F. Police Brass Cash In On Way Out," *San Francisco Chronicle*, February 7, 2011; and Joe Eskenazi, "Heather Fong's Pension: $277,656 Per Year," *SF Weekly*, February 7, 2011.

---

pension benefits earned by past work performed and future pension benefits are contractually protected in California.

A series of cases decided by state court judges, culminating in the 1955 California Supreme Court ruling in *Allen v. City of Long Beach*, established California's "vested rights doctrine" regarding pension benefits.

Alexander Volokh, a professor at the Emory University School of Law, defines the California Rule as thus:

[I]n California (and some other states), the courts give constitutional protection not only to the amount of public employees' pensions that has been earned by past service, *but also* to employees' right to keep earning a pension based on rules that are at least as generous for as long as they stay employed.[6] (Emphasis in original.)

Pensions once promised are a "vested contractual right" that cannot be diminished, not even for work not yet performed, without equal alternative compensation. In *Allen*, the state Supreme Court found that any "changes in a pension plan which result in disadvantage to employees should be accompanied by comparable new advantages."[7]

A public-sector employee has, according to the California Supreme Court, "the primary right to *receive* any vested pension benefits upon retirement, as well as the collateral right to *earn* future pension benefits through continued service, on terms substantially equivalent to those then offered"[8] when he or she was hired.

Jack Beermann, professor of law at Boston University School of Law, has emphasized that some California court decisions have held it permissible to eliminate future pension accruals in the interest of government financial flexibility and control. Though not completely settled, it is safe to say, however, that California courts generally hold to a relatively strict application of the California Rule.[9]

With few exceptions, the pension formula in effect on the date of hire becomes a contract between the government agency and the employee for all service the worker will provide and the contract cannot be impaired unless offset by a new benefit of comparable value.

---

6. Alexander "Sasha" Volokh, "The 'California Rule' for Public-Employee Pensions: Is It Good Constitutional Law?" *The Volokh Conspiracy* and *Washington Post*, February 4, 2014.

7. Allen v. City of Long Beach, *45 Cal. 2d 128 (1955), at 131*.

8. Volokh, "The 'California Rule.'"

9. Jack M. Beermann, "The Public Pension Crisis," *Washington and Lee Law Review* 70, no. 3 (January 2013), 3–94. See pp. 41–42 and 57–60 for discussions on the California Rule and relevant California court decisions.

There is considerable controversy regarding whether California courts ruled properly when they established the California Rule and, if not, what the best rule should be. But the rule has generally been the legal basis for pension protections in California since the 1950s. There have been recent court challenges to the vested rights doctrine (more on this later).

The next chapter examines how funds are amassed to pay pension benefits.

2

How Are Pension Funds Amassed?

LIKE ALL DEFINED-BENEFIT (DB) pension systems, California's DB plans receive their funding from payroll contributions from the employee and from the employer (the government agency). It is important to note, however, that all contributions—employee and employer—originate from taxpayers. Pension systems are intermediaries that collect contributions, invest the contributions to generate earnings, and use the proceeds to pay benefits to retirees. It's that simple—in theory.

The contributions are invested in various instruments such as stocks, bonds, and real estate, under the supervision of board members. For example, a thirteen-member Board of Administration runs CalPERS, which had assets worth $295 billion as of September 2014. CalSTRS has a twelve-member board and its assets totaled $181 billion as of February 2014. The 26-member U.C. Board of Regents governs the UCRP, which had assets worth $53 billion as of June 2014. Board members oversee management of the funds and decide where funds are invested.

Board members are either political appointees, elected by plan members, or ex-officio members (the State Treasurer and State Controller are ex-officio members of both the CalPERS and CalSTRS boards).

Defined-benefit pension systems work as intended when employer and employee contributions plus investment earnings equal promised benefits (and administrative expenses). This is the defined-benefit pension equation:

Employer & Employee Contributions + Investment Earnings
= Promised Benefits

During the past 20 years, for example, for every dollar paid in CalPERS pension benefits, CalPERS's employer members contributed 21 cents, employees contributed 15 cents, and the remaining 64 cents came from investment earnings.

When total proceeds fall short of promised benefits, a pension fund deficit is created. A pension deficit is also called an *unfunded liability*: defined as the difference between what a pension plan promises to pay (its estimated liabilities) and the money accumulated to fulfill those promises (its estimated assets). In other words, an unfunded liability is an estimate of the amount, in excess of assets, needed to pay pension benefits earned up to that time, but not yet paid.

Of course, assets will change based on many factors including contribution levels and investment performance. Contributions are adjusted based on a variety of factors including salary raises, total payroll increases, and cost-of-living increases. And liabilities will change based on many factors including benefit levels and increasing lifespans. So an unfunded liability is a moving target and it is unrealistic to think there will never be times with unfunded liabilities.

The relevant question, therefore, is whether an unfunded liability is manageable long-term or whether it has grown to dangerous and unsustainable levels.

The next chapter looks at the health of California's public pension plans. The numbers speak for themselves and reveal dangerous underfunding and unsustainable pension debts.

3

California's Massive Public Pension Unfunded Liabilities

California's Statewide Public Employee Pension Systems

CALIFORNIA HAS SIX statewide defined-benefit public pension systems: Judges' Retirement System I, Judges' Retirement System II, Legislators' Retirement System, CalPERS, CalSTRS, and UCRP. The latter three are the biggest systems.

The pension obligations of these six systems are massive: $613 billion in fiscal year 2013, according to the U.S. Census Bureau.[1] Pension obligations increased $21 billion in one year alone, from 2012 to 2013. The assets of these pension systems totaled $473 billion, or only 77 percent of obligations.

The role of California officials is to make sure that obligations and assets keep pace such that no dangerous unfunded liabilities emerge. As Governor Jerry Brown has said: "There is no doubt that we are going to have to adjust our pensions so that money coming in is going to be equal to what we can expect what the money going out will be. It's not even a matter of higher math. It's fifth-grade arithmetic."[2]

---

1. See *State-Administered Defined Benefit Pension Systems* (Washington, DC: U.S. Census Bureau, 2013), data released August 2014. The present value of pension obligations is taken from public records of the pension systems. The discount rates were 7.5 percent to 7.75 percent.

2. *Bloomberg Businessweek*, "California Pension Changes to Require Voter Approval, Brown Says," October 13, 2011.

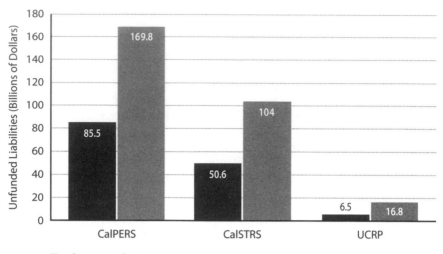

Source: Joe Nation, *Pension Math: How California's Retirement Spending Is Squeezing the State Budget* (Stanford: Stanford Institute for Economic Policy Research (SIEPR), December 13, 2011), 19.

Figure 3.1. Massive unfunded liabilities at California's three largest state-operated public pension funds (fiscal year 2011)

The numbers presented in this section show that state officials have flunked arithmetic when it comes to managing the pension funds, and this exposes California residents to extreme risk.

Figure 3.1 shows the unfunded liabilities of California's three largest pension systems—CalPERS, CalSTRS, and UCRP—at a point in time that permits comparisons across multiple assessments. The solid black bars are the unfunded liabilities *as calculated by each pension plan itself*—these are the government's own numbers.

All three systems self-reported massive unfunded liabilities—UCRP $6.5 billion, CalSTRS $50.6 billion, and CalPERS $85.5 billion. According to the Big Three's own calculations, the state should have had $143 billion more in the bank in 2011 just to pay benefits that have already been earned. And despite several years of strong stock-market performance since 2011, the self-reported unfunded liability has fallen only $7 billion to $136 billion today ($57 billion for CalPERS, $71 billion for CalSTRS, and $8 billion for UCRP).[3] This represents catastrophic mismanagement by California officials. And more significantly, the Big Three's funding ratios are dangerously low.

When a pension system has an unfunded liability, one measure of health is its funding ratio (available assets divided by liabilities). A ratio of 100 percent means that the pension system has sufficient assets to pay all of the accrued benefits owed. Some argue that a funding ratio of 80 percent or more is adequate, but the American Academy of Actuaries calls this a "myth": "Pension plans should have a strategy in place to attain or maintain a funded status of 100 percent or greater over a reasonable period of time."[4] The reason for this strongly worded admonition is that investment markets fluctuate wildly over time and commitment by government officials to full contributions often weaken over time, making anything less than an explicit goal of 100 percent funding a dangerous path. A lower funding ratio implies that a pension system has a greater potential not to pay its promised benefits. Moody's Investors Service considers funding ratios a good tool for determining whether a pension system is at risk of running out of money.[5]

Using each fund's own numbers, every system's funding ratio was dangerously low (see solid black bars in Figure 3.2). CalSTRS's assets, for example, equaled only 70 percent of benefits accrued in 2011. Today, the self-reported funded status of CalSTRS (67 percent) and UCRP (80 percent) each deteriorated from 2011, whereas CalPERS improved (77 percent).[6] In the private sector, pension plans are labeled "at risk" if their funded status falls below 80 percent. Even plans funded above 80 percent can be in danger.

---

3. See the pension funds' most recent comprehensive financial reports, 2013–14.

4. American Academy of Actuaries, "The 80% Pension Funding Standard Myth," *Issue Brief,* July 2012, 1.

5. Mary Williams Walsh, "Ratings Service Finds Pension Shortfall," *New York Times,* June 28, 2013.

6. See the pension funds' most recent comprehensive financial reports, 2013–14.

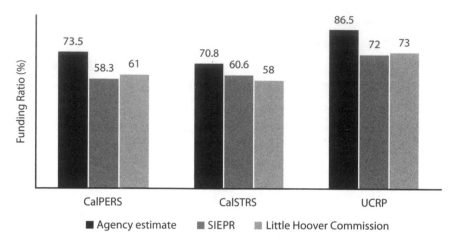

Sources: **Joe** Nation, *Pension Math: How California's Retirement Spending Is Squeezing the State Budget* (Stanford: Stanford Institute for Economic Policy Research (SIEPR), December 13, 2011), 17–18; and Little Hoover Commission, *Public Pensions for Retirement Security* (Sacramento: Milton Marks Commission on California State Government Organization and Economy, February 24, 2011), ii.

Figure 3.2. Dangerously low funding ratios at California's three largest state-operated public pension funds (fiscal year 2011)

The American Academy of Actuaries warns: "A plan with a funded ratio above 80 percent (or any specific level) might not be sustainable if the obligation is excessive relative to the financial resources of the sponsor, if the plan investments involve excessive risk, or if the sponsor fails to make the planned contributions."[7] The goal should always be 100-percent funded. By this measure, California's Big Three public pensions are dangerously underfunded, putting current and future taxpayers at risk.

In 2008, the Employee Retirement Income Security Act (ERISA)—the federal law that sets minimum standards for private-sector pension plans—was amended to add restrictions on private pensions with funding ratios below specified levels. For example, if the funding ratio falls below 60 percent, private pensions must freeze plan benefits regardless of collective-bargaining agree-

---

7. American Academy of Actuaries, "The 80% Pension Funding Standard Myth," 2.

ments. And as Stanford University Professor Joe Nation notes: "A funded status of less than 80 percent precludes systems [in the private sector] from improving benefits or making payments in accelerated forms (such as the lump-sum option within UCRP) that are otherwise available. None of these restrictions applies to public-sector pension systems."[8]

The bottom line is that officials at California's public pensions are permitted to engage in behavior that would be considered criminal under ERISA if done by officials overseeing private-sector pensions.

Government pension plans are exempt from most ERISA provisions, including all provisions related to reporting and disclosure, funding, vesting, and plan termination insurance (ERISA Titles I and IV). Under ERISA, private-sector pension plans must use conservative rates of return when calculating the present value of their future pension liabilities. As a result, private pensions tend to be sustainable and reasonable.[9] State and local pension plans, on the other hand, are governed by standards set in state constitutions, state laws, local ordinances, court decisions, the common law dealing with trusts, and individual plan documents.[10] Government pension plans, therefore, tend to be more varied and complicated than private-sector plans.

The True Health of California's Big Three Public Pension Systems

The official numbers self-reported by the pension plans tell only part of the story. The true picture is much worse.

Moody's Investors Service, the Governmental Accounting Standards Board (GASB, pronounced "gas-bee"), and the vast majority of economists believe

---

8. Joe Nation, *Pension Math: How California's Retirement Spending Is Squeezing the State Budget* (Stanford: Stanford Institute for Economic Policy Research, December 13, 2011), 15.

9. Ed Ring, "Forming a Bipartisan Consensus for Public Sector Union Reform," *Fox and Hounds*, January 29, 2014.

10. Pension Review Board, *Retirement Benefits in the Public and Private Sectors—A Comparison of Trends, Regulatory Environments, and Related Issues*, Research Paper No. 13–002 (Austin, TX: Pension Review Board, August 2013), 13.

Table 3.1. CalPERS, CalSTRS, UCRP, and private-sector
actuarial assumptions and methods

Assumption or Method	CalPERS	CalSTRS[a]	UCRP	Private Sector
Discount rate (percent)	7.75	7.75[b]	7.5	Roughly 6 or less (current)
Amortization period (years)	30[c]	30	30[d]	7
Asset valuation method: smoothing recognition period (years)	15	3	5	2
Asset corridor	20 percent	None	None	10 percent

a DB program only.

b Reduced in 2010 from 8.0 percent.

c Open for gains and losses, except those incurred in FY 2009–FY 2011. 20 years for unfunded liability attributable to changes in plan provisions or actuarial assumptions.

d Increased from 15.

Source: Joe Nation, *Pension Math: How California's Retirement Spending Is Squeezing the State Budget* (Stanford: Stanford Institute for Economic Policy Research (SIEPR), December 13, 2011), 16.

that the financial methodology used by California's public pensions (and virtually all public pensions in the country) has been deeply flawed. There is almost no dispute among academic economists on this point.[11] These flaws systematically overstate assets and understate liabilities so public pensions appear to be healthier than they are.

The Stanford Institute for Economic Policy Research (SIEPR) compared the actuarial assumptions and methods used by CalPERS, CalSTRS, UCRP, and the private sector (see Table 3.1).[12]

The public pension plans use a higher discount rate than private plans. The discount rate is the assumed rate of return on investments and the rate ap-

---

11. Alicia H. Munnell et al., *The Funding of State and Local Pensions: 2012–2016* (Chestnut Hill, MA: Center for Retirement Research at Boston College, July 2013), 1 and 3.

12. This section draws on Nation, *Pension Math*, 16.

plied to future liabilities to arrive at their present value. A higher discount rate increases asset values and lowers liabilities, making the plans look healthier than they are. Slight differences in discount rates can make a huge difference in expected asset and liability values, dramatically impacting required pension contribution rates.

Finance theory teaches that the appropriate discount rate reflects the riskiness of the liabilities, not the riskiness of the assets.[13] Given the current legal protections for California's public pension benefits, the State Budget Crisis Task Force said, "Most researchers believe the risk of nonpayment is low, and some even believe benefits should be treated as risk free."[14] Social Security actuaries use 2.9 percent as the annual real longer-term default-risk-free discount rate.[15] The appropriate real discount rate, therefore, should be in the range of 3 percent to 4 percent, the current market rates on so-called risk-free government bonds, not the 7-percent-plus used by the public pension funds.

Returning to Table 3.1, the amortization period is the assumed number of years required to make extra contributions to eliminate any unfunded liabilities. Ideally, the amortization period should equal the average remaining tenure of employees. A longer amortization period reduces the amount of extra "catch-up" contributions that must be made today. These public pension systems use a dramatically longer amortization period than the private sector: 30 years versus 7 years. If used in the private sector, this amortization period would be considered criminal under ERISA.

The "smoothing" period allows investment losses to be spread over many years rather than using today's market value of the assets. A higher number of years allow current market losses to be buried in an average. CalPERS uses

---

13. See, for example, George Pennacchi and Mahdi Rastad, "Portfolio Allocation for Public Pension Funds," *Journal of Pension Economics and Finance* 10 (2011), 221–45.

14. State Budget Crisis Task Force, *Report of the State Budget Crisis Task Force* (New York: State Budget Crisis Task Force, July 31, 2012), 34.

15. Office of the Chief Actuary, *The Long-Range Economic Assumptions for the 2013 Trustees Report* (Washington, DC: Social Security Administration, May 2013).

a 15-year smoothing period, while the private sector uses a much more prudent 2-year period.

Finally, the asset corridor is the percentage amount by which asset values are allowed to diverge from the market value for reporting purposes. A narrower corridor provides a more realistic picture of the current financial condition of the pension fund. The private sector uses a 10-percent corridor, while CalPERS uses 20-percent and CalSTRS and UCRP use none.

As Stanford professor Joe Nation has concluded: "In short, public pension systems utilize assumptions and methods supporting a consistent theme of understating liabilities, overstating assets, and pushing costs into the future."[16] This has allowed California's public pensions to hide the true extent of the funding problem from the public.

California's public pensions present overly optimistic conclusions by using rosy assumptions and methodologies that are largely prohibited by law in the private sector and would land private-sector pension administrators behind bars. When the same standards are applied to California's public pensions that are required in the private sector, funding ratios plummet and unfunded liabilities soar.

Stanford economists estimated the unfunded liabilities using the more prudent assumptions (market value of assets, 16-year amortization period, and 6.2 percent discount rate—the rate used by investment guru Warren Buffett for Berkshire Hathaway's pension plans). The true unfunded liability for CalSTRS increases by 106 percent: from $50.6 billion to $104 billion. UCRP's unfunded liability increases 159 percent, and CalPERS's rises 98 percent—its unfunded liability jumps to $170 billion (see Figure 3.1, the light-gray bars).

All told, the Big Three's unfunded liabilities equal $290 billion or about $23,800 per California household[17] or $7,600 per California resident. State pension expenditures climb to an equivalent of nearly 20 percent of general fund expenditures when the more prudent discount rate of 6.2 percent is used.[18] Keep

16. Nation, *Pension Math*, 15.
17. Nation, *Pension Math*, 19.
18. Nation, *Pension Math*, 39.

in mind, pension expenditures are funds not available long-term for education, social services, infrastructure, or debt reduction.

All of the Big Three's funding ratios also drop to critical levels using the more prudent assumptions, especially CalPERS's at 58 percent (see Figure 3.2, the three middle bars).

Some claim that these are "political numbers" intended to push a "reform agenda." The problem with this argument is that the revised numbers are simply the result of applying the same methodology used in the private sector for the proper way to value and manage pension funds. In fact, if this methodology isn't used in the private sector, plan sponsors can face criminal penalties.

The Stanford findings are further reinforced by California's nonpartisan Little Hoover Commission, a state oversight agency, which reported similar funding ratios: 73 percent for UCRP, 61 percent for CalPERS, and 58 percent for CalSTRS (see Figure 3.2, the three light-gray bars).[19]

California's statewide public pension plans are also unhealthy compared to other states. Based on a recent comparison of the statewide public pension plans in all fifty states, California has the highest unfunded liabilities—more than two times higher than second-place Ohio.[20] California has the tenth-highest per capita unfunded liabilities at $16,840 per resident, and the thirteenth-highest unfunded liabilities as a percentage of gross state product at 32 percent. California does have the fourteenth-best funding ratio across all fifty states, but that is not saying much since the report calculates California's funding ratio at a dismal 42 percent, less than half the 100 percent funding level recommended by the American Academy of Actuaries. Illinois ranks last in this category at 24 percent funded.

All told, the revised numbers present a sobering picture of the true financial health of California's largest public pension systems. There are no plausible

19. Little Hoover Commission, *Public Pensions for Retirement Security* (Sacramento: Milton Marks Commission on California State Government Organization and Economy, 2011), ii (it only reports funding ratios, not unfunded liabilities).

20. Cory Eucalitto, *Promises Made, Promises Broken—The Betrayal of Pensioners and Taxpayers* (Glen Allen, VA: State Budget Solutions, September 2013).

assumptions that make these pension systems sustainable. Even if the Big Three pension funds earn an optimistic annual investment return of 7.5 percent forever, all three plans are underfunded by an aggregate $136 billion, *meaning they are unable to pay their promised benefits.*[21]

The Consolidated Finances of California's Public Pension Systems

The previous analysis looked at California's Big Three state pension funds. But what does the picture look like across all of California's government employee pension funds?

The California State Controller's office consolidates the financial statements of every state and local government employee pension fund in California. According to the most recent published report, California's state and local public pensions had liabilities of $762 billion, assets of $604 billion, total unfunded liabilities of $158 billion, and a funding ratio of 79 percent, far below the 100 percent standard set by the American Academy of Actuaries and three percentage points less than the prior fiscal year.[22] Figures 3.3 and 3.4 (see the first bars) show the State Controller's numbers for consolidated unfunded liabilities and the resulting funding ratio.

The State Controller's numbers, however, are calculated by the pension systems using flawed assumptions and methodologies as discussed above. What happens when the numbers are calculated using Moody's new rules?

In response to public pension crises across the country, Moody's Investors Service, which rates the creditworthiness of state and local governments, has implemented new rules to evaluate public pension funds.[23] Moody's lowered

---

21. Nation, *Pension Math*, 39.

22. John Chiang, *Public Retirement Systems Annual Report* (Sacramento: California State Controller Office, May 2013).

23. Marcia Van Wagner, *Adjustments to U.S. State and Local Government Reported Pension Data* (New York: Moody's Investors Service, April 2013).

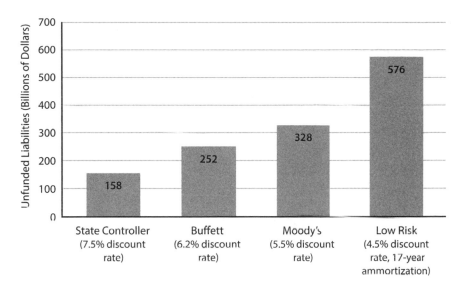

Sources: John Chiang, *Public Retirement Systems Annual Report* (Sacramento: California State Controller Office, May 2013); and Ed Ring, *How Lower Earnings Will Impact California's Total Unfunded Pension Liability* (Tustin: California Public Policy Center, February 2013).

Figure 3.3. The consolidated unfunded liabilities for every state and local government employee pension fund in California under various scenarios

the discount rate to the level of high-grade corporate bonds, similar to the rate private pension systems use. And they eliminated "smoothing" of investment losses and instead value pension assets at current market values. Moody's also requires local governments to include unfunded pension liabilities on their balance sheets for the first time, which is long overdue.

Ed Ring with the California Public Policy Center reassessed the numbers using Moody's new rules.[24] He lowered the discount rate to 5.5 percent and revalued the actuarial accrued liability according to Moody's new criteria. Total unfunded pension liabilities skyrocket to $328 billion and the funding status of California's consolidated state and local government pension plans

---

24. Ed Ring, *How Lower Earnings Will Impact California's Total Unfunded Pension Liability* (Tustin: California Public Policy Center, February 2013).

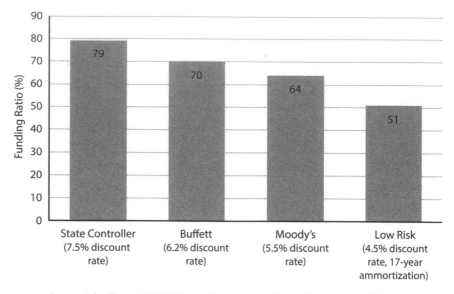

Sources: John Chiang, *Public Retirement Systems Annual Report* (Sacramento: California State Controller Office, May 2013); and Ed Ring, *How Lower Earnings Will Impact California's Total Unfunded Pension Liability* (Tustin: California Public Policy Center, February 2013).

Figure 3.4. The consolidated funding ratio for every state and local government employee pension fund in California under various scenarios

plummets from 79 percent to 64 percent (see Figures 3.3 and 3.4, the third bars). California's pension debt is more than two times higher than official estimates using Moody's new rules.

Ring noted: "[I]f a fund is 50 percent funded instead of 100 percent funded, it cannot survive by hitting its return on investment target of 7.5 percent [assuming no contribution increases], because it is earning that 7.5 percent on half as much money as it needs. It has to earn 15 percent just to stay at 50 percent funded."[25] So not only are California's pension funds not within prudent bounds at 79 percent, they are much worse under Moody's new rules, which peg the actual funding status at 64 percent.

---

25. Ring, *How Lower Earnings.*

Figures 3.3 and 3.4 also report the results using a discount rate of 6.2 percent, or what Stanford professor Nation calls an average historical return on investment of a "Blended 20th Century Fund." And Figures 3.3 and 3.4 list the results using the long-term "risk-free" Treasury bond rate of 4.5 percent and a 17-year amortization period.[26]

Under these distinct, but completely plausible alternative scenarios, *unfunded liabilities increase up to nearly four times the State Controller's numbers.* Many economists consider a risk-free rate of about 4.5 percent to be the appropriate discount rate since under current California law pension benefits must be paid. Using this rate, annual investment returns must average 9 percent forever just to remain 51 percent funded, all else being equal. Some California pension officials now publically admit this is unrealistic. CalSTRS's management said:

CalSTRS earned an approximate 1.84 percent one-year return on a performance basis in fiscal year 2011–12, well below the actuarial assumed rate of 7.5 percent. According to the June 30, 2011, actuarial valuation for the DB Program, the gap between the value of assets and the value of its obligations, or funding gap, has grown to approximately $63.8 billion. *CalSTRS estimates it cannot invest its way out of its projected funding shortfall.*"[27] (Emphasis added.)

CalSTRS admits it cannot invest its way out of this problem.

According to the Legislative Analyst's Office (LAO): "[T]o fully fund CalSTRS in 30 years without changes in contributions or benefits, [annual] investment returns would need to average roughly 10 percent over this period. We agree with CalSTRS that such a high rate of return over a long period is

---

26. Stanford University Professor Joshua Rauh, a pension specialist, has argued that the correct discount rate for public pension funds is 4.5 percent (see *Pension Crisis Solution: Shared Pain*, Fox Business interview, January 23, 2014).

27. California State Teachers' Retirement System, *CalSTRS Building Financial Growth: Comprehensive Annual Financial Report for the Fiscal Year Ended June 30, 2012* (West Sacramento: CalSTRS, January 2013), 26.

very unlikely to occur."[28] Over the past 15 years, the annual time-weighted investment rates of return have been 5.4 percent for CalPERS, 5.8 percent for CalSTRS, and 5.2 percent for UCRP—all well below their actuarial rates of return.[29]

California's Independent Pension Systems for Government Employees

In addition to California's six state-operated defined-benefit government employee pension systems, many California governments and districts operate their own pension systems.

Twenty county retirement systems operate under the parameters of the California County Employees' Retirement Law of 1937 and are similar to the large statewide pension systems in many respects.[30] The "1937 Act" counties are Alameda, Contra Costa, Fresno, Imperial, Kern, Los Angeles, Marin, Mendocino, Merced, Orange, Sacramento, San Bernardino, San Diego, San Joaquin, San Mateo, Santa Barbara, Sonoma, Stanislaus, Tulare, and Ventura. There are also dozens of other independent systems that operate under rules separate from the 1937 Act.

Stanford economists looked at the funding status for each of California's twenty-four largest independent public pension systems.[31] These twenty-four systems are not members of any of California's six statewide pension systems. Independent systems collectively hold more than $150 billion in assets, and if combined, these independent systems would rank behind CalPERS as the

---

28. Legislative Analyst's Office, *Addressing CalSTRS' Long-Term Funding Needs* (Sacramento: LAO, March 20, 2013), 9.

29. Adam Tatum et al., *Unsustainable California: The Top 10 Issues Facing the Golden State* (Stanford: California Common Sense, Stanford University, June 11, 2014), 23.

30. Robert Palmer, *Prepared Statement of Robert Palmer for the Conference Committee on Public Employee Pensions*, (Sacramento: State Association of County Retirement Systems, April 13, 2012).

31. Evan Storms and Joe Nation, *More Pension Math: Funded Status, Benefits, and Spending Trends for California's Largest Independent Public Employee Pension Systems* (Stanford: Stanford Institute for Economic Policy Research, February 21, 2012).

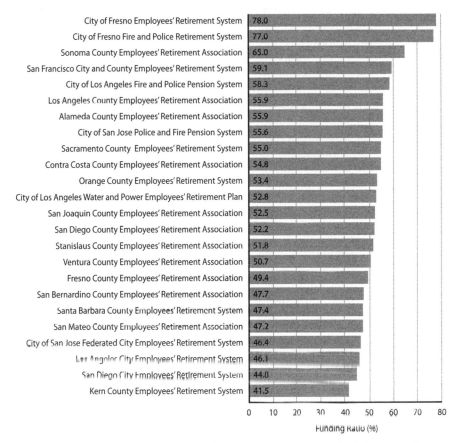

Source: Evan Storms and Joe Nation, *More Pension Math: Funded Status, Benefits, and Spending Trends for California's Largest Independent Public Employee Pension Systems* (Stanford: Stanford Institute for Economic Policy Research, February 21, 2012), 13.

Figure 3.5. The low funding ratios of California's largest independent pension systems for government employees

second largest pension system in the country. The twenty-four systems account for more than 99 percent of independent system assets in California.

Figure 3.5 shows that none of the twenty-four systems have a funding ratio at or above 80 percent, and twenty-one of the twenty-four systems have ratios below 60 percent. The aggregated funding ratio for all twenty-four systems is a dismal 53 percent. The ratios are calculated appropriately using a market value basis for assets and an approximate risk-free discount rate of 5 percent.

The Kern County Employees' Retirement Association has the lowest funding ratio at 41.5 percent. The pension system for the city of San Jose is not much better at 46.4 percent. The unfunded liability of San Jose's two city-run pension systems is nearly $3 billion. Annual pension costs in San Jose soared from $73 million to more than $245 million from 2002 through 2012, consuming 20 percent of the general tax fund.[32] The funding ratio in Los Angeles and San Diego are both worse than San Jose. The aggregated unfunded liability for the 24 systems is $136 billion.

The two pension plans for the city of Los Angeles are underfunded by $10 billion, using the overly optimistic investment rate assumption of 7.75 percent. Using a more realistic rate of 6 percent—Warren Buffett's recommended discount rate—the unfunded liabilities soar to $17.5 billion.[33] Former Los Angeles Mayor Richard Riordan has said the city's outsized public pension costs could bankrupt Los Angeles by 2017.[34]

Ventura County contributed $162 million to its pension fund in 2013, up from $45 million in 2004—a 260-percent increase in just 9 years.[35] The 2013 contribution figure is 17 percent of the county's budget, up from 1 percent in 1999.

Moody's Investors Service calculated that pension costs among Moody's-rated local governments in California increased an average of 14 percent from fiscal year 2011 to fiscal 2012. It noted: "[A]bsent pension reform, we expect this rate of increase to continue for the next several years."[36]

Unlike states, some cities and counties can declare bankruptcy, which can put pension benefits at risk as bankrupt localities restructure operations

32. Ed Mendel, "Skimming 'Excess' Pension Investment Earnings," *CalPensions*, August 19, 2013.

33. Jack Humphreville, "Will We Have a Pension Tax?" *CityWatch*, February 25, 2014.

34. Richard J. Riordan and Tim Rutten, "A Plan to Avert the Pension Crisis," *New York Times*, August 5, 2013.

35. Anna Bitong, "Taxpayer Group Trying to Get Reform Measure on November Ballot," *Thousand Oaks (CA) Acorn*, January 23, 2014.

36. Thomas Aaron and Eric Hoffmann, "California Pension Reform Proposal Not on 2014 Ballot, a Credit Negative for Local Governments," *U.S. Public Finance: Weekly Credit Outlook* (New York: Moody's Investors Service, March 20, 2014).

and contracts. Judge Steven Rhodes of the U.S. Bankruptcy Court ruled in December 2013 that Detroit may impair pensions in a bankruptcy plan: "The state constitutional provisions prohibiting the impairment of contracts and pensions impose no constraint on the bankruptcy process."[37] Detroit's final restructuring plan, approved by Judge Rhodes in November 2014, cuts the monthly checks of general pensioners by 4.5 percent and eliminates their annual pension COLA increases. Detroit's police and firefighter pensioners will see a reduction in their annual pension COLA from 2.25 percent to 1 percent.[38] Public pensions are no longer ironclad.

Since 2008, four California cities—Mammoth Lakes, San Bernardino, Stockton, and Vallejo—sought Chapter 9 federal bankruptcy protection, largely due to high public pension costs. Placentia and Desert Hot Springs are mulling bankruptcy. Desert Hot Springs devotes nearly 70 percent of the city's budget to its police, especially for police salaries and pension payments to CalPERS.[39] Russell Betts, a Desert Hot Springs city council member, said: "It's obvious we can't continue with salaries and pensions that are in the stratosphere, no matter how much love there is for our police department."[40] Desert Hot Springs, which declared a fiscal emergency in November 2013—a precursor to bankruptcy—is considering eliminating its police department and switching to a cheaper county sheriff contract.[41]

In February 2014, Moody's Investors Service issued a special report on California's local pension situation that urged bankrupt California cities to cut their pension obligations, or risk returning to insolvency down the road.[42]

---

37. *In re City of Detroit, Michigan, Debtor, Opinion Regarding Eligibility*, Case No. 13–53846 (U.S. Bankr., E.D. Mich., December 5, 2013), at 74.

38. Lawrence J. McQuillan, "Detroit Bankruptcy Reveals 401(k)'s Virtues," *USA Today*, August 18, 2014.

39. Tim Reid, "Another U.S. City Mulls Bankruptcy Due to Soaring Wages and Pensions," *Reuters*, November 19, 2013.

40. Reid, "Another U.S. City."

41. Luke Ramseth, "As Public Safety, Pension Costs Rise, Desert Cities Look to Sales Tax Increases," *The Riverside (CA) Press-Enterprise*, July 31, 2014.

42. Gregory Lipitz and Tom Aaron, *Without Pension Relief, Bankrupt California Cities Risk Return to Insolvency* (New York: Moody's Investors Service, February 20, 2014).

Vallejo, for example, which exited a 3-year bankruptcy in 2011, restructured its employee compensation including making significant cuts to retiree healthcare benefits. But Vallejo did little to curb its pension bills largely due to threats of legal action by CalPERS. Because of this, Vallejo is now at risk of a second bankruptcy. Its pension costs, which stand at more than $14 million a year, have increased nearly 40 percent in the past 2 years and are projected to increase another 42 percent over the next 5 years. Meanwhile, Vallejo's roads are littered with potholes, a third of its fire stations are closed, and police staffing is down almost 40 percent while crime surges—all because the budget is being swallowed by rising pension costs.[43]

Stockton's bankruptcy-exit plan, approved in late October 2014, leaves public pensions untouched.[44] Stockton agreed to make its $29 million payment to CalPERS in 2015, which is twice as much as in 2012 when the city declared bankruptcy. It will balloon to $36 million by 2020, or 20 percent of all tax dollars. Moody's Vice President Gregory Lipitz said:

> In California, particularly for municipalities with pensions under the California Public Employees' Retirement System, or CalPERS, bondholders will likely continue to pay a steep price if bankruptcies remain venues for restructuring debt obligations but pension liabilities remain untouched.[45]

San Bernardino has indicated that it might seek pension changes but is still in talks with creditors regarding a recovery plan that does not include pension cuts. The city, however, could use the Detroit federal bankruptcy court decision as nonbinding precedent. CalPERS, invoking the California Rule, is challenging San Bernardino's bankruptcy petition.

---

43. Melanie Hicken, "Once Bankrupt, Vallejo Still Can't Afford Its Pricey Pensions," *CNNMoney*, March 10, 2014.

44. Dale Kasler, "Judge Approves Stockton's Plan to Repay Creditors, Leaving Pensions Intact," *Sacramento Bee*, October 30, 2014; and Wall Street Journal Editorial, "A CalPERS Comeuppance," *Wall Street Journal*, October 7, 2014.

45. Dan Walters, "Moody's Warns Bankrupt Cities They Must Cut Pension Debts," *Sacramento Bee's Capitol Alert*, February 20, 2014.

The Detroit ruling is likely to resonate in Chicago, Los Angeles, New York, Philadelphia, San Bernardino, and many other American cities where the rising cost of pensions has been crowding out spending for public schools, police departments, and other traditional public services.[46]

The numbers speak for themselves. Many municipal pension systems in California, like their statewide counterparts, are financially unsustainable as currently configured and are putting more local governments in peril of bankruptcy.

The exposure of California residents to unfunded public pension liabilities is massive and not sustainable long-term under any plausible assumptions. To their credit, some fund managers now publicly admit it. State, county, and city pension systems are well below the funding levels considered safe by the American Academy of Actuaries. Some local governments have already declared bankruptcy. Others are on the brink.

Greater transparency through Moody's and GASB's new pension reporting rules, and associated downgrades in credit ratings, will pressure lawmakers to get more money from taxpayers, further cut government services, or, in some cases, enter bankruptcy.[47]

The next chapter looks at how California got into this mess.

---

46. Regarding the plight of New York City's public pension finances, see David W. Chen and Mary Williams Walsh, "New York City Pension System Is Strained by Costs and Politics," *New York Times*, August 3, 2014.

47. See page 61, note 76, for a discussion on GASB's new pension accounting rules.

4

What Are the Major Drivers of the Pension Problem?

REGARDLESS OF WHOSE numbers you rely on, California's public pensions are in poor financial health and unsustainable long-term without meaningful changes. Some California cities have declared bankruptcy because of pension costs, and others are considering it.

This chapter provides a history lesson: When did the unfunded-liability problems emerge and what factors created the pension crisis? The answers lie in reckless decisions by politicians and pension officials as well as macroeconomic developments that amplified these poor decisions. Irresponsible decisions were made by lawmakers in both political parties—it has been a bipartisan failure.

The key policy failures can be highlighted with the help of the defined-benefit pension equation presented earlier:

$$\text{Employer \& Employee Contributions} + \text{Investment Earnings}$$
$$= \text{Promised Benefits}$$

Four variables affect the health of any defined-benefit pension plan: (1) employer contribution amounts, (2) employee contribution amounts, (3) investment returns, and (4) promised benefits. History shows that in each area decisions were made that created the unsustainable situation facing California today. The following discussion looks at each of these variables, but first, this simple story will illustrate how all four of these factors tie together.[1]

---

1. The college-education example was adapted from Storms and Nation, *More Pension Math*, 4.

Assume there are two families saving for a child's college education. Both expect to need $200,000 (the promised benefits) for tuition and living expenses in 16 years. And each family considers the child's college education as essential; thus, the future payments are mandatory. Accordingly, both discount the $200,000 at a low-risk rate such as the interest rate on long-term California bonds, roughly 5 percent.

Family A actually does invest in California bonds at 5 percent, which requires an investment (total contribution) today of $122,783 (=$200,000/(1.05)^{16}$).

Family B thinks it can do better by investing in stocks, and it expects an annual rate of return of 7 percent. To meet the future obligation, Family B invests today only $67,747 (=$200,000/(1.07)^{16}$).

Notice that these different approaches lead to very different current contribution requirements: Family A's is $122,783 versus Family B's at $67,747. Family A can be nearly certain that its current investment will guarantee receipt of the $200,000 needed in 16 years. But this conservative approach requires a greater initial contribution.

Family B expects the same outcome of $200,000, but its approach is riskier because stocks are more volatile; thus, it does not provide the same guarantee. In fact, based on historical experience, Family B has only a 50 percent chance of achieving the needed $200,000 because returns are often not as high as Family B predicted. Note that the amount owed by each family in 16 years is identical. The only difference is the certainty, or risk, of achieving the goal.

Family B contributed less money upfront but expects to have the needed funds in 16 years through higher returns. But this strategy offers a greater chance of not achieving the goal.

Notice that if the total needed in our illustration were to increase above $200,000, the families would have to either increase their current contributions or engage in a riskier—and assuming successful—investment strategy to achieve the higher goal.

This simple college-education example illustrates how California's public pensions got into the mess they're in today: The pension funds implemented riskier approach B but contributions and investment returns proved to be too

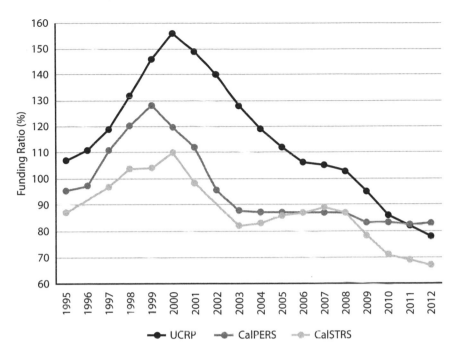

Sources: California Public Employees' Retirement System, *Comprehensive Annual Financial Report: Fiscal Year Ended June 30, 2001* (Sacramento: CalPERS, December 14, 2001), 76; California Public Employees' Retirement System, *Comprehensive Annual Financial Report: Fiscal Year Ended June 30, 2013* (Sacramento: CalPERS, January 2014), 132; Milliman, *Defined Benefit Program Actuarial Valuation as of June 30, 2012* (Seattle: Milliman, March 26, 2013), 26; University of California, *Retirement System 2012–2013 Annual Financial Report* (Oakland: University of California Office of the President, October 9, 2013), 19; University of California, *Final Report of the President's Task Force on Post-Employment Benefits* (Oakland: Office of the President, July 2010), 159; and The Segal Company, *Annual Actuarial Valuations for the University of California Retirement Plan and Its Segments and for the 1991 University of California Public Employees' Retirement System Voluntary Early Retirement Incentive Program,* November 15, 2012, 5.

Figure 4.1. The health of California's Big Three pension funds has been declining since the late 1990s

low, yielding insufficient investment earnings to pay ever-growing benefits. Now to the history lesson.

Today's public pension crisis did not happen overnight. As Figure 4.1 shows, the downward trend began in the late 1990s, well before the Great Recession. Since then, funding ratios for the Big Three have fallen almost without exception, even using the government's more rosy, yet flawed, assumptions.

Though the pension problem has been developing over time, it remains a problem of "simple arithmetic," as Gov. Brown said. Let's look at some of the critical milestones driving California's pension crisis.

Insufficient Employer and Employee Contributions

Before discussing contribution drivers of the pension crisis, it is important to understand pension funding in more detail.[2]

The "normal cost" of pension funding is the portion of the present value of pension benefits plus administrative expenses that is allocated to a given year, and is calculated using one of six standard actuarial cost methods.

The most common method used in the public sector to fund normal costs is the "entry age normal cost" approach, which attempts to create level contributions throughout the working career of the employee, either a level dollar amount or a level percentage of payroll, to fund a member's total plan benefit over the course of his or her career.

The entry age method allocates the present value of benefits for each member on a level basis over the earnings of that member from the age of entry into the pension plan to the expected age at retirement.

The assumed retirement age minus the entry age is the amount of time to fund a member's total benefit. Generally, the older a member is at hire, the greater the entry age normal cost because there is less time to earn investment income to fund the future benefits.

Typically, the normal cost is a level percent of payroll ("normal cost rate") and is usually split between the employer, that is, the government agency, and the employees according to the terms of the collective-bargaining agreement.

---

2. For an excellent overview of pension funding, pension accounting, and terminology see Pension Committee of the American Academy of Actuaries, *Fundamentals of Current Pension Funding and Accounting for Private Sector Pensions Plans* (Washington, DC: American Academy of Actuaries, July 2004).

For example, under the entry age normal method, UCRP's current normal cost is 17.6 percent of covered payroll.[3]

The state's "normal cost" pension contributions are adjusted every year based on a variety of factors, including salary raises, total payroll increases, and COLA increases.

Another key cost is a pension plan's "annual required contribution" (ARC), which is equal to the sum of (1) the employer's share of the normal cost (defined previously), and (2) the amount needed to amortize any unfunded liability over a period of not more than 30 years. The latter amount is an additional "catch-up" payment needed to make up any shortfall due to negative past experiences or plan changes. For example, the state is paying extra to CalPERS for the 24-percent investment loss suffered during the Great Recession. More increases will occur in 2015 and beyond.

An unfunded liability is often the result of underfunding (i.e., failure to pay the normal cost plus any other increase in accrued liability), but there are three principal reasons why even a plan that has always paid the full ARC may have unfunded liabilities at a point in time.[4]

First, actual experience always differs from the actuarial assumptions, and any resulting actuarial losses mean that the actuarially projected ARC was not what was needed in reality, thus creating an unfunded liability. Pension spiking, in particular, contributes to unfunded liabilities since each year that an estimate of higher-than-current salary for plan participants is not used for ARC purposes results in underfunding that has to be made up after the "spiker" retires.

Second, benefit increases are often made retroactive, especially in public-sector plans, meaning that a more favorable formula is applied to past years of service, thus creating an unfunded liability.

3. Segal Company, *Annual Actuarial Valuations for the University of California Retirement Plan and Its Segments and for the 1991 University of California Public Employees' Retirement System Voluntary Early Retirement Incentive Program*, November 19, 2014, 3.

4. Civic Federation, *Pension Fund Actuarially Required Contributions (ARC)*, Civic Federation Issue Brief (Chicago: Civic Federation, February 14, 2007), 5–6.

Third, many plans had an unfunded liability at inception due to prior service credit for employees, and this original liability might never have been fully amortized.

Because paying the normal cost and amortizing the unfunded liability over a period of 30 years has become a standard for a public pension funding policy, the ARC has become a comparative indicator of how well a public entity is actually funding its pension plan. The Pew Center on the States said: "Making the full or almost full actuarially required contribution in any given year signifies that a state is making a serious effort to pay its bill coming due."[5] Funding at the ARC does not guarantee a funded ratio of 100 percent at any given time, for the reasons discussed. But funding at the ARC long-term will approximate 100-percent funding over the long haul.

There is also a moral dimension to the ARC since funding to the ARC each year prevents pension debts from being pushed too far into the future. Intergenerational equity requires that the current generation pay the full cost of public services provided, which includes total compensation costs.

With these funding terms in hand, it is easy to see where the pension funds went wrong regarding contribution rates. As the dot.com stock market boomed in the late 1990s, the pension funds enjoyed temporary funding surpluses. Politicians and pension officials used this opportunity to cut contributions.

The state's contribution to CalPERS dropped from $1.2 billion in 1997 to about $60 million in 2000. CalPERS cut employer contributions to near zero in some cases.[6] To make up for past underfunding, the state now contributes about $3.5 billion annually and CalPERS enacted higher contribution rates in 2013 and 2014.

The same behavior occurred at CalSTRS. In 2000, Assembly Bill (AB) 1509 cut the state's CalSTRS contribution from 2.6 percent of pay in fiscal year 2000–2001 to 2 percent in 2003–2004. And AB 1509 diverted a quarter of the teachers' pension contribution (2 percent of pay) into a new individual

---

5. Pew Center on the States, *The Trillion Dollar Gap: Underfunded State Retirement Systems and the Roads to Reform* (Washington, DC: Pew Center on the States, February 2010), 15.

6. Mendel, "Skimming 'Excess.'"

investment fund for teachers—the Defined Benefit Supplement Plan (DBSP). According to Ed Mendel with *CalPensions*, AB 1509:

> Emerged from a back-room deal and went directly to the legislative floors, bypassing committee hearings. A brief Assembly floor analysis of AB 1509 in 2000 said: "Fiscal effect: No General Fund effect and no effect to the solvency of STRS; the STRS surplus will absorb the cost of DBSP."[7]

But the "surplus" vanished quickly and proved to be inadequate.

The diversion of money from CalSTRS's defined benefit fund lasted 10 years and totaled $5 billion—but payments from the fund were not reduced.[8] Until 2000, the full amount of the teachers' contribution—8 percent of pay— had been appropriately going into the pension fund.

In each fiscal year since 2001–02, officials have shortchanged CalSTRS by paying less than 100 percent of its full-funding obligation.[9] Worse yet, California lawmakers have paid less than 50 percent of the amount needed to fully fund CalSTRS's pensions in 2011 through 2013.[10]

The State Budget Crisis Task Force, co-chaired by former Federal Reserve Board Chairman Paul Volcker and former New York Lieutenant Gov. Richard Ravitch, looked into CalSTRS's funding in its 2012 report. Table 4.1 presents the findings: CalSTRS's ARC was underpaid by more than $11 billion from 2006 through 2011.

In 2013 alone, the ARC was underpaid by $3.5 billion, the largest skipped ARC in the country,[11] and CalSTRS received only 44 percent of its ARC.

---

7. Ed Mendel, "Brown 'Committed' to Getting CalSTRS Rate Hike," *CalPensions*, January 13, 2014.

8. Ed Mendel, "Brown 'Committed.'"

9. Editorial, "Pay Off Teacher Pension Debt," *San Mateo Daily Journal*, January 10, 2014.

10. Editorial, "Pay Off Teacher Pension Debt."

11. David Crane, "Teachers' Pension Crisis: How It Happened," *U-T San Diego*, March 8, 2014; and David Crane, "As Days Go By: Why Jerry Brown Must Act THIS Year on CalSTRS," *Fox and Hounds*, January 15, 2014.

Table 4.1. CalSTRS's ARC was underpaid by $11 billion from 2006 through 2011 (millions of dollars)

	Annual Required Contribution (ARC)	Actual Employer Contribution	Overpayment (or Underpayment)	Percent of ARC Paid (%)
2006	3,821	2,440	(1,381)	63.9
2007	3,980	2,649	(1,331)	66.6
2008	4,362	2,864	(1,498)	65.7
2009	4,547	2,867	(1,680)	63.1
2010	4,924	2,693	(2,231)	54.7
2011	5,985	2,796	(3,189)	46.7
Six-Year Total	27,619	16,309	(11,310)	59.0

Source: State Budget Crisis Task Force, *Report of the State Budget Crisis Task Force* (New York: State Budget Crisis Task Force, July 31, 2012), 38.

It doesn't take an actuarial expert to figure out that CalSTRS will *never* pay off its debt with this funding approach. It is equivalent to owing $10,000 on a credit card and not even making the minimum payment each month—the interest on the debt grows faster than the amount paid, so the balance owed keeps growing. Economists call this a negative amortization repayment schedule.

CalSTRS's funding formula can be changed only by the state legislature. Currently, school districts give CalSTRS a sum equal to 8.25 percent of teacher pay, teachers have 8 percent deducted from their paychecks for pensions, and the state government contributes about 5 percent. CalSTRS's members do not make contributions to Social Security while employed as teachers in California and, thus, do not directly qualify for Social Security benefits at retirement. The absence of participation in Social Security is often mentioned to justify the higher pension contribution rates for teachers compared to some other job classifications.

CalSTRS estimates that the cost to fully fund the teachers' pension debt will be $4.2 billion in the coming year and more in each subsequent year. The longer it takes the legislature to increase contributions, the higher the total cost will be to eliminate the unfunded liability due to foregone investment returns compounded over time. As noted by David Crane, a Democrat and former special advisor to California Governor Arnold Schwarzenegger:

> If CalSTRS's deficit is not addressed, then the next generation will be forced to spend at least $45 billion per year meeting CalSTRS's bills. In other words, either our generation starts paying $4.5 billion per year towards promises we made for services we received or we force the next generation to pay ten times as much for promises they didn't make and services they won't receive. That's not hyperbole; that's math. It's also injustice.[12]

This pattern of underfunding existed at UCRP as well. In 1990, when UCRP's funding ratio was 137 percent, the Board of Regents suspended both employer and employee contributions to the retirement fund and state legislators stopped allocating funds for the UCRP.[13]

After a 20-year "pension contribution holiday," contributions began again for both UC and its employees in April 2010, after its funding ratio had plummeted to 75 percent. And for the first time in more than 20 years, state legislators voted to appropriate state money—$90 million in fiscal year 2012–13—for the UCRP.[14]

The devastating impact of the pension holiday was admitted in a September 2010 UC report: "Had contributions been made to UCRP during each of the prior 20 years at the Normal Cost level, UCRP would be approximately 120 percent funded today."[15] The pension holiday was reckless and irresponsible. As noted recently by the American Academy of Actuaries, one hallmark of

---

12. David Crane, *An Open Letter to Governor Jerry Brown*, Govern for California, January 6, 2014.

13. University of California Office of the President (UCOP), *The Facts: Contributions to the UC Retirement Plan*, May 2012.

14. University of California Office of the President, *The Facts.*

15. University of California Office of the President, *University of California Post-Employment Benefits—An Overview*, September 16, 2010, 7.

a well-run pension fund is that contributions "should actually be contributed to the plan by the sponsor on a consistent basis."[16] This is an obvious statement, but California pension plans have ignored the obvious, sometimes for decades.

It is also common, but little known, that many California public employees do not contribute anything into their pensions, even when there isn't a so-called pension holiday. This perk is called a "pension pickup," and it can increase taxpayer costs.[17]

For example, workers with the Bay Area Rapid Transit (BART) system have enjoyed a pension pickup until the most recent collective-bargaining contract. Station agents have not had to pay any of their $4,661 average per capita annual CalPERS contribution.[18] Instead, the employer has picked up the tab.

All told, California has been paying only 86 percent of its public pension ARC over the most recent 5-year period of data examined by the Pew Center on the States.[19] The contribution rate was even worse in the last fiscal year Pew examined (2010): California paid only 75 percent of its ARC.[20]

Even assuming the pension funds would meet their rosy actuarial assumptions, especially the generous expected rates of return on their investment portfolios, not enough money has been contributed into the investment portfolios to meet their future benefit obligations. This is a "simple-arithmetic" recipe for disaster. California officials have not made a serious, good-faith effort to establish pension-fund solvency.

---

16. Pension Practice Council of the American Academy of Actuaries, *Objectives and Principles for Funding Public Sector Pension Plans*, American Academy of Actuaries Issue Brief (Washington, DC: American Academy of Actuaries, February 2014), 5.

17. Thomas Peele and Daniel Willis, "'Pension Pickup': Bay Area Taxpayers Foot the Bill for Little-Known Perk," *San Jose Mercury News*, June 24, 2013.

18. Lawrence J. McQuillan, "Time to Unload the BART Gravy Train," *The Beacon*, July 10, 2013.

19. Pew, *Trillion Dollar Gap*, 56.

20. Pew Center on the States, *The Widening Gap: Funding Public Sector Pensions and Retiree Health Care Benefits*, Data Visualizations, June 18, 2012.

Unsuccessful Risky Investment Strategies

California's public pension funds have consistently increased the riskiness of their investment portfolios. This, in turn, has allowed them to increase their actuarial investment return targets, allowing politicians to artificially lower required contributions. These actions have contributed to rising pension debt.

For example, when CalPERS was formed in 1932, it was bound by law to invest only in low-risk U.S. government bonds and municipal bonds. Over time, CalPERS's allowable investments have become riskier.

In 1947, utilities were added to CalPERS's investment portfolio. In 1953, legislation was passed allowing it to invest in real estate. In 1967, common stocks were added, although it could only invest up to 25 percent of its portfolio in these securities. And in 1984, Proposition 21 removed CalPERS's stock limitation. Every change increased the riskiness of CalPERS's investment portfolio[21] and made it more vulnerable to stock market collapses such as the Great Recession.

In his book *Plunder!* journalist Steven Greenhut explained that CalPERS bet big on property at the peak of the real estate bubble, including "some highly risky deals involving vacant land." When the bubble burst, "CalPERS lost 103 percent of the value of its housing investments in one fiscal year" because it had borrowed money—up to 80 percent in some cases—to finance the deals. CalPERS had to pay back the borrowed money because it guaranteed the debts.[22]

Today, CalPERS is placing more investments with risky private equity companies and hedge funds. Public pension expert Leo Kolivakis argues that CalPERS does not have an alternative to riskier investments since it maintains overly optimistic investment assumptions:

---

21. For a detailed timeline see Little Hoover, *Public Pensions*, 11.
22. Steven Greenhut, *Plunder!* (Santa Ana, CA: Forum Press, 2009), 85.

CalPERS can't take its chances with more passive investments because the bond and equity markets are going to have down years. In order to achieve that (reduced) 7.5 percent benchmark return, CalPERS had to construct a portfolio of alternative investments, including private equity, which can meet a benchmark annual return of nearly 30 percent.[23]

CalPERS's investment portfolio has a target allocation of 47-percent equities, 19-percent fixed income, 6-percent inflation-sensitive securities, 12-percent private equity, 11-percent real estate, 3-percent infrastructure and forestland, and 2-percent cash.[24]

Some local pension funds have resorted to direct lending to midsized companies in the United States, Europe, and Asia.[25] These companies need money but are not strong enough to access traditional credit markets. The Orange County Public Employees Retirement System has agreed to loan $450 million, and the Los Angeles County Employees Retirement Association has committed $400 million. The hope is that these high-risk and high-interest-rate loans, which banks have refused to make, will replenish pension funds. But the loan principal could easily be lost.

By increasing the riskiness of the investment portfolio, fund actuaries could assume higher rates of return, which reduced required up-front contributions—something the politicians wanted. The pension funds took on more risk to justify their rate-of-return assumptions. A recent report on this topic concluded: "In the past two decades, U.S. public pension funds uniquely increased allocations to riskier investments to maintain high discount rates . . . thereby camouflaging the degree of underfunding."[26]

---

23. Leo Kolivakis, "CalPERS Strikes Fear Into PE Firms?" *Pension Pulse*, February 20, 2014.

24. PlanSponsor Staff, "CalPERS Adopts New Demographic Assumptions," *PlanSponsor*, February 19, 2014.

25. Mike Reicher, "Pension Board for Public Employees Takes $450 Million Risk," *Orange County Register*, January 23, 2014.

26. Aleksandar Andonov, Rob Bauer, and Martijn Cremers, *Pension Fund Asset Allocation and Liability Discount Rates: Camouflage and Reckless Risk Taking by U.S. Public Plans?* Social Science Research Network, May 1, 2013, 1.

But realized rates have not met the rosy expectations. California's Big Three public pensions assume an annualized rate of return on investments of 7.5 percent, down recently from 7.75 percent. This actuarial target assumes, in effect, that the stock market will double every decade and fixed-income yields will rise without harming current bond portfolios. If done in the private sector, this actuarial investment rate would be considered criminal under ERISA. Even CalPERS's own chief actuary Alan Milligan told a CalPERS's committee that the system has only a 50 percent chance of meeting the 7.5 percent target over the next 19 years.[27] The chance only goes up to 54 percent if the investment target is dropped to 7.25 percent.

Put another way, the Big Three assume that they will outperform the average portfolio return in the twentieth century by 2.1 percent every year for decades. Recent history demonstrates otherwise.

For example, over the past 15 years, the annual time-weighted investment rates of return have been 5.4 percent for CalPERS, 5.8 percent for CalSTRS, and 5.2 percent for UCRP.[28]

Despite these actual returns, the pension funds stubbornly hold to their high actuarial rates of return and discount rates. CalSTRS's own actuary concludes there is more than a 50 percent chance that the fund will not meet its investment return target.[29] Maintaining these rosy targets helps politicians to divert tax revenue to other programs, but it is financially reckless and irresponsible, ultimately hurting younger generations.

The differences between the assumed and realized rates of return might not seem large, but as the college-education example illustrated, relatively small differences in investment returns compounded annually make a huge difference on the contributions needed up front to keep the programs on track to meet funding goals, or, conversely, on how big deficits will be when

---

27. Oakland Tribune Editorial, "Once Again, CalPERS Ignores Its Own Expert's Advice," *Oakland Tribune*, March 13, 2012.

28. Tatum et al., *Unsustainable California*, 23.

29. David Crane, "Memo to Legislature: No Time for Half Measures on CalSTRS," *Sacramento Bee*, February 19, 2014.

contributions are not increased sufficiently. According to Berkshire Hathaway, the 100-year average annual rate of return for a blended twentieth-century portfolio of equities and fixed income was 6.2 percent[30]—much lower than the rosy rates of return assumed by California's public pension funds.

If CalPERS fails to earn 7.50 percent on its investments, it has the power to increase the required contributions from the government employers of its members. It can cover its losses on the backs of taxpayers and those who rely on government services. In a moment of unguarded honesty, CalPERS's chief actuary Alan Milligan admitted this: "[W]e can ask the employers to make up any shortfall. That's what allows us to invest the way we do," meaning in riskier stocks, private equity, and real estate rather than in risk-free government bonds.[31]

By assuming unrealistically high returns, politicians artificially reduced the pension contributions made each year, which freed up money for other government programs. But this risky approach helped drive pension debt sky-high. The pension funds made ever riskier bets, assuming that in most cases taxpayers would backfill significant losses. When the bets didn't pay off, pension debts escalated, and now the day of reckoning has arrived.

In summary, pension contributions have been too low given the actual investment returns in the market, not the fanciful returns assumed by pension officials. Again, "simple arithmetic"—specifically massive unfunded liabilities—proves that actual rates of return were insufficient, given the level of contributions, to yield the assets needed to meet promised benefits.

Miscalculations of Life Expectancy and Retirement Dates

Miscalculations and inaction on life-expectancy effects and the timing of retirement are also driving public pension debt higher in California.

---

30. Storms and Nation, *More Pension Math*, 4.
31. Ed Mendel, "CalPERS Boosts Cost of Terminating Pension Plans," Calpensions.com, August 22, 2011.

As people live longer in retirement, pension funds must provide benefits for more years. California pension funds have done a poor job of including increased life expectancy into their actuarial calculations. Daniel Borenstein explained:

> Currently, CalPERS studies the mortality data for its members every four years and from that projects how long retirees will live and receive benefits. But those numbers don't account for the expectation that people will live longer in the future; it only considers how long they've lived in the past.[32]

CalPERS has not incorporated dynamic advances in longevity into their life-expectancy actuarial accounting, and neither has any other California pension system.[33] As a result, pension funds are chronically underfunded, driving up pension debt.

Governor Brown's office calculated that CalPERS needs an additional $1.2 billion a year to pay for added pension expenses due to longer life expectancy. By 2028, men retiring at age 55 are expected to live an average of 2.1 years longer and women 1.6 years longer. Brown urged CalPERS to pay for this cost using higher contributions from employers (cities, counties, special districts, and the state) beginning in fiscal year 2014–15 for a 20-year period. Brown wanted the annual increases fully phased in within 3 years.[34]

CalPERS's staff wanted to phase-in full payments over 5 years for all employers, starting in fiscal year 2016–17.[35] The staff was concerned that a quick

---

32. Daniel Borenstein, "Time for CalPERS to Get Real about Life Expectancy," *Contra Costa Times*, January 17, 2014. For more on longevity and how it affects defined-benefit pension funding, see Michael Kisser et al., "Longevity Assumptions and Defined Benefit Pension Plans," Working Paper (January 31, 2014); and Meaghan Kilroy, "New Actuary Tables May Be 'Nail in the Coffin' for DB Plans," *Pensions & Investments*, July 23, 2014.

33. Chris Reed, "Life Expectancy Gains: New Front in California Pension Funding Woes," CalWatchdog.com, January 20, 2014.

34. The figures in this paragraph are in a letter from Governor Jerry Brown to CalPERS's President Rob Feckner, February 5, 2014.

35. Dale Kasler, "CalPERS Poised to Raise Rates, but Not on Brown's Timetable," *Sacramento Bee*, February 13, 2014.

ramp up would add to cities' financial stress and cause drastic service reductions in some communities.

But Brown scolded CalPERS for wanting to delay the contribution increases: "No one likes to pay more for pensions, but ignoring their true costs for two more years will only burden the system and cost more in the long run."[36] Brown contended that delaying implementation of the full-contribution increase would hike pension costs $3.7 billion over the next 20 years.

CalPERS's board has final say on rate implementation, and on February 18, 2014, it voted to increase state contributions by $400 million starting July 1, 2014. The increase will be phased in over 3 years and will ultimately cost an extra $1.2 billion a year, bringing the state's annual CalPERS payment to $4.7 billion. Note that this money going to public pensions will not be available for other general-fund programs such as schools.

CalPERS's board also approved higher contributions for thousands of school districts and local governments but chose to start them in July 2016, with a more gradual 5-year phase-in. School districts and localities currently contribute about $4 billion a year to CalPERS.

The rate hike will cost the city of Sacramento, for example, $12.2 million more a year at the peak of the new rates, according to Sacramento's finance director Leyne Milstein.[37] That's $12 million that won't be going to other city services. It is the equivalent of cutting thirty-four police officers, thirty firefighters, and thirty-eight other employees.[38] This is "service-delivery insolvency" in action.

Pat Morris, then San Bernardino Mayor, responded to the rate increase:

---

36. Letter from Governor Jerry Brown to CalPERS's President Rob Feckner, February 5, 2014.

37. Dale Kasler, "CalPERS Decides to Speed Up Rate Increases for State," *Sacramento Bee*, February 18, 2014.

38. The Press Democrat Editorial, "CalPERS Comes Knocking—Again," *The Press Democrat (Santa Rosa, CA)*, February 24, 2014.

[The pension system] is currently unsustainable for cities and it is increasingly impossible with the prospect of these new inflated CalPERS contribution rates to balance the critical equation of giving our city adequate services and paying these overly generous retirement benefits to these retirees. Without reform . . . more cities will find themselves insolvent—cash insolvent and service insolvent.[39]

Another miscalculation by California's public pension funds has been in estimating when government workers will choose to retire. In 1999, the California legislature and then governor Gray Davis dramatically increased pension benefits and made the increase retroactive (more on this in the next section). The increase in benefits encouraged government workers to retire earlier. CalPERS's actuaries did a poor job of estimating the impact of the benefit increases on the decision to retire, resulting in higher pension debt.

Workers who retire earlier than expected will draw pension checks for more years and will reduce the number of years that some funds are invested. Both effects drive pension debt higher. In the case of CalPERS, significant miscalculations were made.

For example, after the 1999 benefit increases, more than twice as many California Highway Patrol (CHP) officers retired as CalPERS expected. This miscalculation alone will result in state taxpayers having to pay another $31 million a year for CHP pension contributions.[40]

Pension actuaries are not updating assumptions frequently enough, nor are they taking into consideration all information available on life expectancy and the decision to retire. As discussed in the next section, this could be partially due to the "generally accepted practices" that they follow.

---

39. Ryan Hagen, "California's Pension Increases Were Expected, Not Welcomed," *San Bernardino Sun*, February 19, 2014.

40. Daniel Borenstein, "CalPERS Underestimated How Many CHP Would Take Big Pensions," *Contra Costa Times*, January 31, 2014.

Increasing Pension Benefits

In 1932, CalPERS's benefits were "1.43 percent at 65," meaning that a public employee's pension was calculated by multiplying 1.43 percent with the total years of service and then multiplying that result by the final salary to arrive at the annual pension amount eligible at age 65. In 1945, the formula was increased to "1.67 percent at 65." An automatic COLA was added in 1968 followed by a benefit increase to "2 percent at 60" in 1970.[41]

As Figure 4.1 showed, a soaring dot.com stock market in the late 1990s handed California's public pension funds surpluses. At the urging of CalPERS, California lawmakers used the opportunity to give government workers generous pension enhancements.

In 1999, state lawmakers passed, and Governor Gray Davis signed, Senate Bill (SB) 400, a more generous formula for calculating pension benefits for government workers. It created the "2 percent at 55" tier for many state employee classifications. SB 400 also lowered minimum retirement ages and allowed state and local agencies to enhance pension benefits for public safety employees. SB 400 increased CHP pensions by 50 percent, setting a benchmark later used by local police and firefighter unions in their contract negotiations. It allowed CHP officers to retire with up to 90 percent of their pay at age 50. Also, all of these changes could be applied retroactively.

At the time, CalPERS's board claimed in its promotional literature that SB 400 could be implemented "without it costing a dime of additional taxpayer money."[42] The board contended that surplus funds and "superior" stock market returns would cover the additional cost of the higher benefits for at least 10 years. CalPERS, in fact, gave the state a "holiday" from making a substantial contribution to the pension fund during that time.

SB 400 passed with overwhelming support of 70–7 in the Assembly and 39–0 in the Senate, but it quickly created huge pension-funding problems.

---

41. This section's history of CalPERS's benefits borrows from evidence and testimony in Little Hoover, *Public Pensions*, 11–14.

42. Little Hoover, *Public Pensions*, 13.

CalPERS's board learned as early as 1999 that if the fund experienced poor investment returns in the future, then the state would have to increase its payments to CalPERS, a scenario that was soon realized after the dot.com bust, followed by the 2008–09 stock market plunge. SB 400 will cost taxpayers at least $10 billion over 20 years, plus billions more at the local level for similar pension increases.[43]

Tony Oliveira, then president of the California State Association of Counties, a Kings County supervisor, and a member of CalPERS's governing board, told the Little Hoover Commission in 2011 that the "3 percent at 55" formula authorized by SB 400 for public safety officers "moved across agencies like a grass fire."[44] He testified that local officials believed the added costs were covered by investment surpluses and agreed to hike pensions to match benefits offered by other communities. Some counties enhanced benefits prospectively and others retroactively.

SB 400 put in motion a bidding war among government agencies, particularly at the local level, to attract and retain personnel by boosting retirement benefits.

Mr. Oliveira testified that officials, including him, who supported SB 400, did not fully understand the ramifications, and he called SB 400 "one of the worst public policy decisions in the history of California."[45] The *San Diego Union-Tribune* editorial board said: "Passage of such a massive pension spike would have been impossible had CalPERS put an honest price tag on its cost. ... CalPERS has somehow gotten a pass it doesn't remotely deserve—without so much as a mea culpa. Even by Sacramento standards, this is a joke."[46]

Former Governor Gray Davis, who signed SB 400, now says it was a mistake. "The evidence seemed to suggest the state was wealthy enough to afford

---

43. Daniel Weintraub, "Cozy State Pension Deal Costs Taxpayers Billions," *Sacramento Bee*, August 10, 2003.

44. Little Hoover, *Public Pensions,* 14.

45. Little Hoover, *Public Pensions,* 14.

46. *San Diego Union-Tribune* Editorial Board, "The Saga of SB 400: Don't Forgive CalPERS for Its $10 Billion Error," *San Diego Union-Tribune,* May 29, 2007.

it," he said in 2010. "It was part ideology and part math, and the point is the math was wrong, big-time."[47]

The impact of SB 400 was devastating. The *Sacramento Bee* analyzed data from CalPERS's internal annual reports, obtained through a California Public Records Act request, and found the average first-month pension payout for new retirees doubled between 1999 and 2012.[48] CalPERS's deputy chief actuary David Lamoureux has attributed "at least 50 percent" of the payment increase to salary growth and at least 20 percent to the 1999 benefit enhancements.[49]

Ed Ring compared apples to apples and concluded that the 1999 benefit enhancements increased pension payments more than 20 percent. He compared the average annual CalPERS benefit check for a hypothetical, identical public employee working a 30-year career and retiring either before or after SB 400.[50] The average check in 1998 was $37,912. It had risen to $50,958 in 2012, a 34-percent increase.

Now Californians are living with the aftermath of SB 400 as these higher benefits roll through the pension system like a tsunami with each successive wave of retirements. The sudden and massive surge in retirement benefits will not die anytime soon because of the nature of pension accounting and demographics. Long before the Great Recession, lawmakers made changes to California's public pension benefits that devastated funding ratios. The Great Recession merely accelerated the inevitable catastrophe.

The legislature compounded the 1999 policy fiasco with another pension benefit increase passed in 2001. This law allowed local agencies to increase

---

47. Little Hoover, *Public Pensions*, 13.

48. Lawrence J. McQuillan, "California's Pension Tsunami Swells as Pension Benefits Surge," *The Beacon*, September 9, 2013. The average first-month pensions to state police and firefighters nearly tripled. CHP officers' first-month retirement payments more than doubled, as did pensions for local government safety employees.

49. Ortiz, "California Public Pension Payouts Doubled."

50. Ed Ring, *How Much Do CalPERS Retirees Really Make?* (Tustin: California Public Policy Center, February 13, 2014).

the pension formulas for general employees to as high as "3 percent at 60," putting in motion another bidding war.

The track record is no better at CalSTRS. A half dozen CalSTRS benefit increases were enacted around 2000, including a longevity bonus for teachers who reached the 30-year employment milestone during the following 10 years.[51] These increases harmed CalSTRS's financial position, as later admitted by its actuary in April 2013.

Mark Olleman testified to the CalSTRS board: "If we were still operating under the 1990 benefit structure, the plan would be about 88.4 percent funded instead of 67 percent. So the difference between 88.4 percent and 67 percent shows that one of the impacts on the funding of the plan currently is benefits."[52] A full 25 percent of the collapse in CalSTRS's funding ratio from 2000 to 2012 was caused by benefit increases, according to CalSTRS's actuary company Milliman.[53]

In a 2013 report, the nonpartisan LAO scolded California lawmakers for the CalSTRS benefit hikes: "In the future, we advise policymakers to avoid changing pension contributions or benefits based on any short period of strong investment gains."[54] In other words, markets tend to revert to the mean, so do not increase benefits in response to temporary stock-market surges.

Benefit increases have been common at UCRP, too.[55] In 1967 (UCRP began in 1961), pension eligibility at retirement was changed from age 55 and 20 years' service credit to age 55 and 5 years' service credit. In 1971, automatic annual

51. Mendel, "Brown 'Committed'"; and Chris Megerian, "No Easy Fix for California's Teacher Pension Crisis," *Los Angeles Times*, February 20, 2014.

52. Ed Mendel, "CalSTRS Benefit Hikes Big Part of Pension Debt," *CalPensions*, April 15, 2013.

53. Ed Mendel, "Skimming 'Excess' Pension Investment Earnings," *CalPensions*, August 19, 2013.

54. LAO, *Addressing CalSTRS' Long-Term Funding*, 4.

55. The UCRP benefit history is based on Appendix L, "University of California Retirement Plan, an Historical Perspective" in Task Force on Post-Employment Benefits, *The Report of The President's Task Force on Post-Employment Benefits* (Oakland: University of California Office of the President, July 2010).

COLAs were applied to retirement benefits. The following year, the pension formula was increased to "2 percent at 60," rather than age 63.

In 1988, an ad-hoc COLA was approved giving annuitants 75 percent of original UCRP pensions' purchasing power. But perhaps most irresponsibly, during the period that UCRP had a 20-year "pension contribution holiday," 1991–2010, it nevertheless experienced several benefit increases.

In 1990, the minimum retirement age was reduced to age 50 (from 55). The following year, the ad-hoc COLA was increased to give annuitants 80 percent of original UCRP pensions' purchasing power. In 1992, the pension formula was changed to "2.4 percent at 60," and age factors from 50 through 59 were increased. Then in 2001, the pension formula changed to "2.5 percent at 60" (from 2.4 percent), and the public safety members' formula changed to "3 percent at 50." UCRP benefits have been consistently hiked throughout the years.

In summary, what began in 1932 as a program to provide modest pensions to retired government workers has morphed into a system that provides generous benefits to ever-younger retirees. And today's problems are partly the result of misinformation and mismanagement by politicians and pension officials, especially regarding the impact of benefit increases and pension holidays. SB 400 was passed in 1999 based on misinformation supplied by CalPERS's board.[56] And CalSTRS erroneously told the legislature that a decade-long diversion of teachers' contributions would have "no effect to the solvency" of CalSTRS.[57]

The impact of benefit enhancements is now coming home to roost as workers retire who were hired under the more generous formulas, with some retirees receiving six-figure pensions. This is the slow-motion "pension tsunami" in action.

Table 4.2 lists the highest pensions paid by CalPERS to retired California government employees.

56. Bruce Maiman, "All Parties Involved Are Needed to Fix Pension Mess," *Sacramento Bee*, December 10, 2013.

57. Mendel, "Brown 'Committed'."

Table 4.2. The CalPERS's high rollers' club

Name	Monthly Pension	Annual Pension	Employer
Michael D. Johnson	$30,920.24	$371,042.88	County of Solano
Robert Hurst	$27,377.08	$328,524.96	San Diego County Superior Court
Joaquin M. Fuster	$26,226.08	$314,712.96	University of California, Los Angeles
Donald R. Gerth	$24,590.52	$295,086.24	California State University at Sacramento
William Garrett	$24,129.46	$289,553.52	City of El Cajon
David N. Ream	$23,375.33	$280,503.96	City of Santa Ana
James F. Stahl	$23,289.98	$279,479.76	Los Angeles County Sanitation District No. 2
John Schlag	$22,604.16	$271,249.92	University of California, Los Angeles
Glenn D. Southard	$22,596.42	$271,157.04	City of Indio
Randy G. Adams	$22,347.94	$268,175.28	City of Bell

Source: "The Top 10 List," CalPERS database maintained by Fix Pensions First, accessed January 10, 2014. The information was obtained through a California Public Records Act request.

Michael D. Johnson, former Solano County administrator, tops the list with an annual pension exceeding $371,000 for life. Robert Hurst receives more than $328,000 a year, and Joaquin M. Fuster takes home $314,000 annually.

All told, more than 31,000 California government retirees receive pensions in excess of $100,000 a year for life while not working ($100,000 is 71 percent higher than California's 2012 real median household income of $58,328).[58]

58. Hoover Institution, *California Public Pension Solutions: Post Conference Report* (Stanford: Hoover Institution Leadership Forum, February 2014), 4.

These generous pensions feed the growing view among taxpayers and voters that government employees see the public treasury as a personal trough.[59]

Some government retirees also received a "thirteenth check" bonus. When investment earnings exceeded the annual actuarial forecast, retirees in some pension plans received a distribution from that "surplus" in the form of another check. Some government employers also shared in the "windfall." The thirteenth check skimmed money that should have stayed invested in the pension fund. This practice has added to the pension debt facing future generations.[60]

Overall, California has the fifth-highest average annual public pension benefits of any state at $30,886, according to U.S. Census Bureau data.[61] Only six states pay average annual public pensions greater than $30,000. Connecticut is highest at $37,954. But these numbers provide a distorted picture since the methodology relies on a cohort that includes people who retired decades ago under different formulas and people who didn't work full careers. An apples-to-apples comparison is needed.

Fortunately, Andrew Biggs with the Washington, DC–based American Enterprise Institute has done such a comparison and found that the average annual pension benefit for a new full-career retiree from California state government is $61,560.[62] California ranks third highest behind Nevada and Alaska when comparing identical worker profiles across states. To control for potential cost-of-living differences and any effects due to differences in Social Security participation, Biggs also compared across all fifty states *total retirement income* (combined pension and Social Security income) for full-career state government employees to the earnings of full-time employees in each state. California's ratio of 87 percent ranked fourth highest nationally. With

---

59. Little Hoover, *Public Pensions*, 46–47.

60. Mendel, "Skimming 'Excess'."

61. Erika Becker-Medina, *Annual Survey of Public Pensions: State-Administered Defined Benefit Data Summary Report: 2011* (Washington, DC: U.S. Census Bureau, 2012), 6.

62. Andrew G. Biggs, *Not So Modest: Pension Benefits for Full-Career State Government Employees*, AEI Economic Perspectives (Washington, DC: American Enterprise Institute, March 2014), 2 and 4.

or without adjustments, California's public pension benefits are generous and rank in the top four.

The present value of these lifetime retirement benefits for an average full-career California state employee is $1,274,593.[63] It is no exaggeration to say the typical full-career California state employee will retire a "pension millionaire." The typical Californian, however, who must pay for these public pensions, will not have anything close to $1.2 million in a 401(k) or IRA when they retire.

A majority of California's private-sector workers (55 percent) have no employment-based retirement plan. Those who have a defined-contribution (DC) plan will accumulate nothing close to what full-career California state employees receive.

According to Vanguard, a defined-contribution participant age 65 or older has a median DC account balance of $65,193 and mean account balance of $176,696 for a 10-year work period. For DC participants age 55 to 64, the median is $67,239 and the mean is $154,421. Even if a DC participant had three 10-year-tenure plans over a 30-year career at the mean amount (a best-case scenario), on average they still wouldn't have one-half of the amount a full-career California state worker receives. The figures come from Vanguard's defined-contribution plans with more than $500 billion in plan assets. Its full-service defined-contribution business alone serves 1,600 plan sponsors and more than 3 million participants.[64]

The gap between the size of California public pensions and the much lower retirement savings of those who pay for the public pensions cannot be explained or justified on the grounds that private-sector workers receive Social Security benefits and California state workers do not. The majority of California state workers participate in Social Security just like private-sector workers.[65] Also,

63. Biggs, *Not So Modest*, 5.

64. Vanguard Institutional Investor Group, *How America Saves 2013: A Report on Vanguard 2012 Defined Contribution Plan Data* (Valley Forge, PA: Vanguard Group, Inc., 2013), 1 and 39.

65. *Effect of Social Security Coverage on CalPERS Benefits*, SSSAP Bulletin No. 5 (California State Social Security Administrator Program (SSSAP), September 2013).

the net compensation benefit that a median private-sector employee receives from participation in Social Security compared to a public employee with no Social Security coverage is at best 4 percent of wages. This difference does not come close to offsetting the California public pension advantage.[66]

The unfunded liabilities of California's public pensions are self-inflicted and not primarily due to the Great Recession. Most of the critical drivers of the crisis (listed in Table 4.3) were set in motion long before 2008, especially the retroactive benefit increases and the underfunding of contributions urged on or implemented by politicians and pension officials. The downward trend in pension health was apparent as early as the late 1990s and early 2000s. Now taxpayers are being asked to pay for the promises made by public officials who did not set aside enough money to meet these promises. Most of these politicians left office years ago.

The Role Played by Accountants, Actuaries, and Auditors in the Downward Descent

One group often ignored when assessing the pension crisis is financial-control personnel: the accountants, actuaries, and auditors at the pension funds. They all maintain deniability because they follow "generally accepted practices," but the story is more complicated than this.

For example, according to CalPERS's annual report: "The accounting policies used to prepare these financial statements conform to accounting princi-

---

66. Andrew G. Biggs and Jason Richwine, *Overpaid or Underpaid? A State-by-State Ranking of Public-Employee Compensation* (Washington, DC: American Enterprise Institute, April 2014), 40-41. The 4 percent figure is derived using the methodology reported in Biggs and Richwine 2014: Social Security's "money's worth ratio" for a median two-earner couple born in 1973 (the median age of a U.S. worker) is .82. Multiplying .82 by 12.4 percent (the combined Social Security tax) yields 10.168. Subtracting the employee's contribution of 6.2 percent leaves the net compensation benefit from Social Security of 3.968 percent of wages. The benefit is even lower for single workers of either gender. The money's worth ratio of Social Security is the present value of the expected benefits divided by the present value of the expected taxes. A value of less than one for this ratio indicates that, on a present value basis, less money will be received in benefits than will be paid in payroll taxes over the lifetime of that individual or cohort.

Table 4.3. Critical actions that drove California's public pension debt sky-high

---

Funding pension systems below the ARC

Contribution holidays and pension pickups

Increased riskiness of investment portfolios over time

Unrealistically high actuarial rates of return and discount rates

Underestimating the life expectancy of pensioners

Miscalculation of government workers' retirement date

Ever-more generous benefits through formula enhancements, COLAs, and skimming (the 13th check)

Lowering the minimum age of retirement

Retroactive application of more generous benefit formulas

Competitive bidding among government agencies using pension benefits to lure new employees

---

Source: Author Lawrence J. McQuillan.

ples generally accepted in the United States."[67] Moreover: "The basic financial statements are presented in accordance with the guidelines of the Governmental Accounting Standards Board (GASB)."[68]

The same deniability comes from CalPERS's actuaries. The chief actuary Alan Milligan said in the annual report: "The actuarial assumptions and methods used for funding purposes meet the parameters set for disclosures presented in the Financial Section by Governmental Accounting Standards Board...."[69] The same goes for the auditors.

CalPERS's annual report said its internal Office of Audit Services "performs assurance and consulting work consistent with the Institute of Internal Auditors' International Standards for the Professional Practice of

---

67. California Public Employees' Retirement System (CalPERS), *Comprehensive Annual Financial Report: Fiscal Year Ended June 30, 2012* (Sacramento: CalPERS, January 2013), 3.

68. CalPERS, *Comprehensive Annual Financial Report: Fiscal Year Ended June 30, 2012*, 4.

69. CalPERS, *Comprehensive Annual Financial Report: Fiscal Year Ended June 30, 2012*, 124.

Internal Auditing."[70] And the independent external auditor, Macias Gini & O'Connell, LLP, said: "We conducted our audit in accordance with auditing standards generally accepted in the United States of America,"[71] which are consistent with the standards contained in *Government Auditing Standards* issued by the Comptroller General of the United States.

To the extent that California's pension crisis was driven by an inaccurate picture of the extent of the problem, the cause does not appear to be financial-control personnel ignoring generally accepted practices. Rather, the problem is in the practices themselves that result in actuarial estimates that are "smoothed, stretched, averaged, backloaded, and otherwise spread across time," as described by the *New York Times*.[72]

The accountants and actuaries followed the "Generally Accepted Accounting Principles" (GAAP) for state and local governments established by the Governmental Accounting Standards Board (GASB). GASB is a nonprofit professional association, not a government agency. Almost all state and local governments produce financial statements according to GASB's rules. The accountants' and actuaries' job of producing accurate financial statements was made more difficult, in fact, by such things as pension spiking, which injects greater uncertainty into pension calculations. But they appear to have followed accepted practices.

The true culprit was GASB's rules, which allowed billions of dollars of unfunded government pension debt to accumulate unreported to the public. As John G. Dickerson of the California Public Policy Center said: "The Fatal Flaw is that pension expenses that create unfunded pension debt are reported in the future as that debt is paid. That's absurd—the payments of a debt eliminate the debt, they don't create it. Unfunded pension debt is created by pension expenses in the past—most of which have never been reported to the

---

70. CalPERS, *Comprehensive Annual Financial Report: Fiscal Year Ended June 30, 2012*, 210.

71. CalPERS, *Comprehensive Annual Financial Report: Fiscal Year Ended June 30, 2012*, 14.

72. Mary Williams Walsh, "Panel Seeks Greater Disclosures on Pension Health," *New York Times*, February 24, 2014.

people."[73] The accepted practices and lack of transparency allowed lawmakers to hide from the public the true extent of the problem.

An extreme example of this is Detroit. Using actuarial standards, Detroit's pension fund was shown to be healthy on paper just before the city's bankruptcy, when the pension fund turned out to be actually billions of dollars in deficit.[74] In reality, Detroit's municipal debt was around $18.2 billion and public employee pensions and retiree healthcare obligations accounted for $9.2 billion of the liabilities, or about $13,000 per Detroit resident.[75]

GASB's rules allowed unfunded pension debt to be hidden and reported as a lower amount than it should have been. GASB recently changed the rules on how governments must calculate and report pension finances. The changes are mostly for the better.[76] The new rules will provide a more accurate picture of the financial position of state and local governments. But the new rules do not "tell" governments how much they should pay into their pension funds.

The next chapter explains why government officials have allowed pension problems to escalate and why lawmakers have not solved the problems.

---

73. John G. Dickerson, *How New Rules from Moody's and GASB Affect the Financial Reporting of Pensions in Seven California Counties* (Tustin: California Public Policy Center, March 2013).

74. Walsh, "Panel Seeks Greater Disclosures."

75. Riordan and Rutten, "A Plan to Avert the Pension Crisis."

76. Under GASB's old rules, pension assets are reported on an actuarially smoothed basis, the discount rate is the long-run expected rate of return, and the annual required contribution (ARC) serves as the metric to measure whether a pension-plan sponsor is meeting its funding obligations.

Under GASB's new rules: (1) pension assets will be reported at market value rather than actuarially smoothed; (2) projected benefit payments will be discounted at a lower rate closer to the risk-free interest rate; (3) the entry age normal/level percentage of payroll will be the allocation method used for reporting purposes; (4) net pension liability will be listed as real debt on financial statements for the first time; and (5) net pension assets related to pension obligation bonds will be removed from financial statements.

5

Why Did Lawmakers Allow This Problem To Worsen and Why Have They Not Solved It?

CALIFORNIA'S PUBLIC PENSION problems, at all levels of government, have grown over time, yet lawmakers in both political parties have been unwilling to fix the problems. There are five primary reasons for the lack of political resolve in the face of this crisis.

The first is the "Wimpy Syndrome." To quote J. Wellington Wimpy of Popeye fame: "I'll gladly pay you Tuesday for a hamburger today." Everyone prefers to have a benefit today and postpone payment into the future. Many voters and taxpayers are happy to get public services without paying the full cost, meaning the cost that includes the public employee pension costs. Lawmakers are happy to dole out higher pension benefits without increasing contributions. They kicked the pension can down the road, but with each kick, pension costs grew. CalSTRS's unfunded liability, for example, has increased $22 million a day with inaction.[1]

Second, elected officials knew pension recipients and their families would be more likely to vote for them if they increased pension benefits. Lawmakers sought votes and campaign contributions by pandering to special interests with higher pension benefits.

There is nothing new in this, but pensions are particularly well suited for vote buying because the full costs of higher pensions are not realized initially—the pension tsunami takes years, if not decades, to swell. Lawmakers

---

1. Katie Orr, "Assembly to Tackle Teacher Retirement Fund Debt," *Capital Public Radio*, January 29, 2014.

can make pension promises today and the full cost is pushed into the future, whereas base-pay increases today raise costs immediately.

Voters and taxpayers tend to be more aware of present-day costs than future costs. Economists call this effect *fiscal illusion*. The present-day cost of pension enhancements seems low to voters and taxpayers, so there is little opposition to benefit increases. Imperfect information and fiscal illusion allowed California lawmakers to play the vote-buying game numerous times with pensions, and with few negative consequences until recently.

Third, using higher pension benefits to buy votes is particularly attractive in California because the state has term limits, forcing any legislator elected today to leave office after 12 years. Term limits encourage elected representatives to buy votes now using higher pensions knowing they will be out of office when voters become aware of the true costs and the pension bill is due. There are no legislators in office today that voted for the disastrous SB 400 in 1999, yet now Californians are stuck paying the bill.

Fourth, the old saying is one death is a tragedy, a thousand deaths is a statistic—meaning the public relates more to an individual story than to a mass number. People who support higher pensions understand this and have worked to limit information on individual pensions to reduce the emotional impact tied to the unfairness. A $576 billion pension deficit is a statistic; a $371,000 annual pension for Michael Johnson of Solano County seems inherently more unfair because it is personalized. Supporters of higher pensions know this and have worked to block transparency, citing such things as the privacy of pensioners or safety concerns.

For example, CalPERS had plans to launch a searchable Internet database containing names, pension-payment amounts, final employers, years of service, and other information. The database was put on hold in July 2013 when pensioner groups such as the Retired Public Employees Association of California complained to legislators that it would "give someone enough information to prey on elders."[2]

---

2. Michael Hiltzik, "Should CalPERS Post Pensioners' Financial Data Online?" *Los Angeles Times*, July 19, 2013.

In January 2014, the database plan died when CalPERS's spokesman Brad Pacheco said: "Next month, staff will report to the Board that we no longer believe the intended benefits of posting the database on our website outweigh the risks and concerns to our members and that we should not move forward with our previous plans."[3] Keeping the public in the dark is a concerted strategy. Only through costly and tedious California Public Records Act requests can the public know personalized pension information.

Fifth, returning to the college-education illustration in the previous chapter, remember that Family B could contribute much less money into the college fund today by adopting a riskier investment strategy with a higher assumed rate of return. That is what California lawmakers have done with pensions: They contributed a smaller amount of money up front and assumed it would earn a high rate of return for decades, but it did not happen.

This risky approach, however, allowed California lawmakers to promise generous pension benefits to public employees and contribute less money up front to the pensions. The lower contributions, in turn, freed up money to be spent on other programs. It was sold as a win for politicians, a win for pension recipients, and a win for taxpayers and consumers of other government services. But it proved to be a house of cards built on a faulty foundation of politically-motivated rosy assumptions that is now collapsing.

It is important to note that both Democrats and Republicans played the pension game, allowing California's public pension problems to escalate.

In 1991, Republican Governor Pete Wilson raided $1.6 billion from the CalPERS "surplus" reserve to help close a state General Fund budget deficit. In 1999, the Democratic-controlled state legislature passed, and Democratic Governor Gray Davis signed, SB 400, a major pension benefit enhancement that Davis has now admitted was "wrong, big-time" and another government official called "one of the worst public-policy decisions in the history of California."[4]

---

3. Jon Ortiz, "Officials Poised to Officially End CalPERS' Pension Database Project," *Sacramento Bee,* January 13, 2014.

4. Little Hoover, *Public Pensions,* 14.

Members of both political parties have made reckless and irresponsible financial decisions regarding California's public pensions because, ironically, these decisions advanced politicians' short-term interests. Perverse incentives motivated politicians to blow a hole in the state's defined-benefit public pensions and to hide the hole with the help of GASB rules.

As unfunded pension liabilities pile up, it is clear that recent reforms have been inadequate. And the capacity and willingness to finance pension debts has weakened in many jurisdictions as California's economy struggled after the Great Recession and debts increased. Meaningful reforms will only happen if imposed from the outside by voters, or approved from the inside by lawmakers feeling sufficient pressure from taxpayers, voters, consumers of government services, and the credit markets.

As an example of credit markets exerting influence on pension decisions, global financial ratings company Fitch downgraded the $213 million in pension-obligation bonds that Kern County issued in 2003 to shore up its county employees' pension system.[5] One factor influencing the downgrade decision was the expectation of rising pension costs. The downgrade will increase the county's future borrowing costs. Any credit rating downgrade compromises the ability of state and local governments to issue general obligation bonds and issue more specific bonds for schools, roads, sewers, and other public services.

The next chapter explores the immorality of California's public pension crisis.

---

5. James Burger, "Ratings Agency Fitch Downgrades Kern County Pension Bonds," *Bakersfield Californian*, February 27, 2014.

6

The Immorality of California's Public Pension Crisis

WHEN UNFUNDED PENSION liabilities exist, as they do in California, current recipients of government services are not paying the full cost of those services. In other words, current recipients are enjoying the government services, but they are not contributing enough money today into the pension funds to fully pay for the pension benefits of the government workers who provided the services.

A long-term funding ratio below 100 percent means future generations will pay for the pension expenses incurred by governments to provide services to people in the past. The lower the funding ratio, the greater the burden shifted forward to future generations. This is how pension arithmetic works. And it raises important questions of fairness and morality.

First, why should young people be forced to pay for services they never enjoyed? It is selfish and immoral for the current generation to burden future generations with debt and taxes to pay for services they never consumed such as past police protection or past public school teachers. Also, it is impossible for future generations to participate in current tax, spending, and debt discussions, even though they must bear the burden of decisions arising from such discussions.[1] Nobel laureate economist James M. Buchanan summed it up:

---

1. It is possible that some public spending, such as building or repairing roads, benefits future generations. But these spillover benefits are largely "inframarginal" positive intergenerational externalities that result as unintended consequences of spending decisions intended to benefit the current generation. Also, regardless of any positive intergenerational externalities, future generations obviously did not participate in discussions or consent to past spending

"'Taxation without representation' is literally descriptive of the plight of those who will face the debt-burden overhang in future periods."[2]

California's approach to public pension funding produces massive intergenerational inequity. The 30-year amortization period alone guarantees burden shifting to future generations.

It is immoral to force future Californians to pay hundreds of billions of dollars for services they never agreed to, services they never received, or debt they never consented to. Current recipients of government services should put adequate money aside to fully pay for pension benefits. As it now stands, future generations are on the hook to pay for California's pension mess. And as shown in Chapter 3, the intergenerational resource transfer stands to be huge: billions of dollars that will be taken from future generations to pay for services wanted by past generations. California's current approach to pension funding will crush future generations under a mountain of debt. This is unfair and immoral.

Second, another impact is that future generations will be forced to forego government services that their parents and grandparents enjoyed, or accept lower quality services, in order to pay for past pension promises they didn't consent to. This "service-delivery insolvency" is as real as financial insolvency. Future generations should not be expected to receive fewer government services only because past generations selfishly chose not to pay the full cost of their services.

Michael Fletcher of the *Washington Post* described the process of service-delivery insolvency in San Jose:

> Here in the wealthy heart of Silicon Valley, the roads are pocked with potholes; the libraries are closed three days a week, and a slew of city

---

that affects them and might have preferred a different mix of spending. See James E. Alvey, "James M. Buchanan on the Ethics of Public Debt and Default," *Journal of Markets & Morality* 14, no. 1 (Spring 2011), 91.

2. James M. Buchanan, *The Economic Consequences of the Deficit* (1986), in *The Collected Works of James M. Buchanan*, Vol. 14 (Indianapolis: Liberty Fund, 2000), 467.

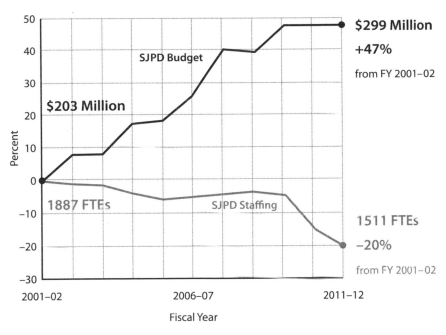

Source: City of San Jose, Office of Mayor Chuck Reed, "Slides from Mayor Reed's Presentation to the U.C. Berkeley Institute of Governmental Studies," 2012.

Figure 6.1. Service-delivery Insolvency in San Jose

recreation centers have been handed over to nonprofit groups. Taxes have gone up even as city services are in decline, and Mayor Chuck Reed is worried. The source of Reed's troubles: gold-plated pensions that guarantee retired city workers as much as 90 percent of their former salaries. Retirement costs are eating up nearly a quarter of the city's budget, forcing Reed (D) to skimp on everything else.[3]

San Jose experienced 10 years of service cuts. Figure 6.1 shows service insolvency in the San Jose Police Department (SJPD). From fiscal year 2001–02 through 2011–12, the SJPD budget increased nearly 50 percent while staffing

---

3. Michael A. Fletcher, "In San Jose, Generous Pensions for City Workers Come at Expense of Nearly All Else," *Washington Post*, February 25, 2014.

fell 20 percent. Over time, more money has been eaten up by police pensions, leaving less money to hire and retain police officers and to provide other city services. In one picture, this graphic shows why current pensions are unsustainable. Voters, taxed to their limits, are refusing to increase taxes to pay for growing pension costs, leaving local officials only two options: cut services further or file for bankruptcy protection. The California Rule takes the direct approach of fully modifying pensions off the table.

In 2014, San Jose announced the layoff of 100 more police officers, which Mayor Reed said was due to the pension debt.[4] This is service-delivery insolvency in action and why current pension costs are politically unsustainable at the state level and in many local communities.

Money spent on pensions is money that can't be spent on traditional government services or kept by taxpayers for their own spending or saving priorities. Future generations are being deprived of services that their parents and grandparents benefited from, including higher-quality schools, safer streets, community parks, and neighborhood libraries. Pension costs for California's public school districts will more than double in the next 7 years, consuming money for classroom instruction and school facilities.[5]

The Oakland Police Department has stopped responding to forty-four categories of crimes because of police cutbacks due to rising pension costs.[6] As pension costs rise, police service deteriorates and crime escalates. Any pension system that forces this tradeoff is immoral by threatening life and property.

In San Francisco between 1999 and 2011, pension costs increased faster than spending on public assistance (which grew at 6.1 percent per year on average), public protection (5.4 percent), health and sanitation (2.6 percent),

---

4. Steven Greenhut, "Oddly Upbeat California Pension Reformers Regroup in Sacramento," *PensionTsunami.com*, March 25, 2014.

5. Chuck Reed, "Pension Costs Draining California School Budgets," *U-T San Diego*, July 25, 2014.

6. Lawrence J. McQuillan and Adriana N. Vazquez, "Private Security Rise Is People's Response to Decline in Police," *Oakland Tribune*, January 12, 2014.

public ways and facilities (0.17 percent), recreation and cultural services (4.1 percent), and miscellaneous functions (3.8 percent).[7]

In Orange County between 1999 and 2011, pension costs increased faster than county spending on education (5.3 percent), on public assistance (5.7 percent), on public protection (5.2 percent), on health and sanitation (6.2 percent), and on public ways and facilities (6.7 percent).[8]

The projected increase in pension spending at the University of California is more than triple the current U.C. research budget ($585 million), eight times that of academic support libraries ($236 million), and 50 percent greater than current student financial aid ($1.256 billion).[9]

Pension costs in Santa Barbara County consume $90 million of the annual budget and grow at a double-digit rate, while deferred maintenance of $18 million a year on buildings, grounds, and equipment goes unmet.[10]

As Detroit has shown, budget-balancing service cuts lower the quality of life in a community, chasing the good residents away and further eroding the tax base. In 1950, Detroit was a thriving city of more than 1.8 million people. Now it has 700,000 people, having lost 61 percent of its population.[11] Raising taxes, if politically possible, discourages business development, further reducing revenues and undercutting expected levels of public services. For example, about 40 percent of Detroit's streetlights do not work, despite crime on the rise.[12]

Skyrocketing public pension costs across California are crowding out spending on other government services, leading to service-delivery insolvency followed by, in some cases, bankruptcy. But long before bankruptcy,

---

7. Storms and Nation, *More Pension Math*, 22.

8. Storms and Nation, *More Pension Math*, 26.

9. Nation, *Pension Math*, 38.

10. Henry Dubroff, "The Case for a Defined Contribution Pension System in California," *Pacific Coast Business Times*, February 7, 2014.

11. Kate Linebaugh, "Detroit's Population Crashes," *Wall Street Journal*, March 23, 2011.

12. Michael Snyder, "25 Facts about the Fall of Detroit That Will Leave You Shaking Your Head," *The Economic Collapse*, July 20, 2013.

service cuts occur on a painful scale. This can be death of communities by a thousand cuts.

As observed by Joshua Rauh, a Stanford University finance professor and pension authority, local communities tend to explore significant pension reform or bankruptcy when about 20 percent of tax revenue goes solely to pension contributions.[13]

But it is not only policy wonks who understand the burden of today's public pensions. A recent statewide survey by the Public Policy Institute of California found that 85 percent of likely voters in California think public pension costs are "a problem" or "a big problem" for state and local government budgets.[14] As more people become aware of service insolvency, the option of playing politics with pensions runs out.

Finally, why should taxpayers, especially the poor and working class, be asked to pay for public pensions that are more generous than anything available in the private sector for performing identical jobs?

U.S. companies have terminated more than 17,000 DB plans in the past 20 years, including IBM and Hewlett Packard in 2005.[15] The value of assets held in employer DC plans, excluding IRA balances, has exceeded the value of assets held in employer DB plans since the mid-1990s.[16] According to data analyzed by the Employee Benefit Research Institute (see Figure 6.2), only 3 percent of private-sector workers in the United States in 2011 participated

---

13. Joshua Rauh interviewed by Fox Business reporter Adam Shapiro, "Pension Crisis Solution: Shared Pain," January 23, 2014.

14. Mark Baldassare et al., *Californians and Their Government*, PPIC Statewide Survey (San Francisco: Public Policy Institute of California, January 2014), 16.

15. Ken Mandler, "Land a State Job and Become an Instant Millionaire," *Capitol Weekly*, 2004. Also see Barbara A. Butrica et al., *The Disappearing Defined Benefit Pension and Its Potential Impact on the Retirement Incomes of Baby Boomers*, Social Security Bulletin 69, no. 3 (2009).

16. John Broadbent, Michael Palumbo, and Elizabeth Woodman, *The Shift from Defined Benefit to Defined Contribution Pension Plans: Implications for Asset Allocation and Risk Management* (Basel, Switzerland: Committee on the Global Financial System, Bank for International Settlements, December 2006), 14.

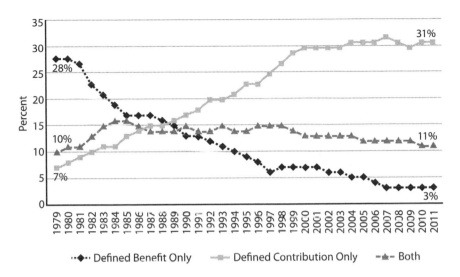

Source: Employee Benefit Research Institute, *FAQs about Benefits—Retirement Issues: What Are the Trends in U.S. Retirement Plans?* (Washington, DC: Employee Benefit Research Institute, 2013).

Figure 6.2. The percentage of private-sector workers in DB plans
has fallen dramatically since 1979

only in a guaranteed DB pension plan. In contrast, 89 percent of public-sector workers participate in a traditional DB pension plan, including almost all government employees in California.[17] Meanwhile, most private-sector workers in California (55 percent) do not participate in *any* employment-based retirement plan.[18]

There are several questions that naturally arise: Why should the California Constitution protect a public-employee benefit that most Californians lost long ago? Why should public employees be given unique, even exalted, status? Also, why should taxpayers and voters employed in the private sector

17. Alicia H. Munnell, Jean-Pierre Aubry, and Mark Cafarelli, *Defined Contribution Plans in the Public Sector: An Update*, State and Local Pension Plans Number 37 (Chestnut Hill, MA: Center for Retirement Research at Boston College, April 2014), 6.

18. Fletcher, "In San Jose, Generous Pensions."

(including union members) pay for generous public pensions that make the typical full-career California government employee a pension millionaire, while such pensions are unavailable to them for doing the identical job?

Overall compensation disparities between public and private employees in California are large. Two of the most systematic studies of California compensation disparities were completed by Jason Richwine at the Heritage Foundation and Andrew Biggs at the American Enterprise Institute. In the first study, the economists did a full accounting of state and local public employee compensation in California, applying rigorous statistical techniques.[19]

After controlling for other factors that could influence pay differences such as years of education, experience, and hours worked, the researchers found that state government workers earn 10.2 percent less in wages than similar private-sector workers. Local government workers earn 0.6 percent less than private workers. Combining state and local workers together yields a wage penalty of 3.7 percent. But wages are only a part of total compensation.

Next the researchers looked at retiree healthcare, job security, and pension benefits, often overlooked by other studies. Richwine and Biggs concluded:

> [P]roperly accounting for retiree health benefits and defined-benefit pension plans generates a public compensation premium of around 15 percent. The additional job security granted to public-sector employees is equivalent to an approximately 15 percent increase in public compensation, meaning that the total public-sector pay premium in California may be as high as 30 percent.[20]

In a second, more recent study, Biggs and Richwine concluded that California state workers receive a 30-percent compensation premium from their

---

19. Jason Richwine and Andrew G. Biggs, *Are California Public Employees Overpaid?* (Washington, DC: Heritage Foundation, March 17, 2011).

20. Jason Richwine and Andrew G. Biggs, *Are California Public Employees Overpaid?* 7. Richwine and Biggs corrected for differences in Social Security participation using data from the U.S. Bureau of Labor Statistics collected through the federal government's *Employer Costs for Employee Compensation* survey.

government pensions alone, compared to identical private-sector workers in California.[21]

The higher taxes needed to pay for generous pensions and higher overall compensation for California public employees, in turn, deprive people in the private sector of money for their own retirement savings. This is unfair. People at all income levels, but especially the poor, should not be forced to pay total compensation for public employees that is more generous than a worker in the private sector could receive *for doing the identical job*, but this is occurring in California.

San Jose Mayor Chuck Reed explained the inequity in an interview with the *Washington Post*:

> This is one of the dichotomies of California: I am cutting services to my low- and moderate-income people . . . to pay really generous benefits for public employees who make a good living and have an even better retirement.[22]

Fairness also dictates, however, that California governments fully pay for pension benefits earned by workers for past work performed. It would be immoral for governments to default on pension benefits already earned by workers for past labor services. This is a key principle guiding the reforms presented in Chapter 8. Adherence to this principle, however, does not preclude reducing pension benefits for future work not yet performed.

The refusal to seriously confront the pension debt is both fiscally irresponsible and unjust. As noted by moral philosopher Samuel Gregg:

> [A] situation of inexorably increasing debt and a failure to confront its moral and economic causes can slowly corrode our personal sense of

21. Andrew G. Biggs and Jason Richwine, *Overpaid or Underpaid? A State-by-State Ranking of Public-Employee Compensation* (Washington, DC: American Enterprise Institute, April 2014), Figure 3, 64.

22. Fletcher, "In San Jose, Generous Pensions."

responsibility for our freely undertaken obligations and severely tempt us to live in a fantasy world of moral and fiscal unreality.

Such attitudes don't just weaken economies. The damage to our personal moral well-being, not to mention entire societies' moral ecology, is immeasurable. [23]

Californians ought not encourage further moral decay. The current generation should step up and pay its pension bills for services it enjoyed so future generations will not have to cover pension debts for services that they did not consent to and should not be expected to pay.

---

23. Samuel Gregg, "Debt, Finance, and Catholics," *Religion & Liberty* 21, no. 2 (Spring 2011), 10–11.

SECTION II

The Solutions

SECTION II PRESENTS a comprehensive blueprint to resolve California's public pension crisis and similar crises in other states and localities across America. Chapter 7 discusses the economic arguments regarding why pensions can be a useful part of a competitive employee-compensation package, even in the public sector where "residual claimants" to profits do not explicitly exist.

Given the reasons for providing pensions to government workers, Chapter 8 presents the crucial elements of a comprehensive solution to California's public pension problems. The first three reform recommendations would stop the problem from getting worse and fully fund the pension plans without severe hardships on future generations.

The final three reform recommendations would guarantee that California never repeats this crisis. The reforms would fully fund accrued benefits in exchange for switching all current and future government employees to sustainable defined contribution pension plans going forward and requiring voters to preapprove any proposed plan changes that increase financial obligations.

7

Why Offer Pensions At All?

FROM 1850, WHEN California became a state, to 1932, California did not offer its government workers a pension. In 1930, California voters approved an amendment to the California Constitution to allow pensions to be paid to state employees. The following year a state law was passed to establish a state worker retirement plan. In 1932, the "State Employees' Retirement System" (SERS) began.[1]

A partial solution to California's public pension problems would be for state and local governments to stop offering pensions as of a specific date. After all, for 82 years California did not allow pensions for state workers, so it could do so again. But there are several economic reasons why pensions can be a useful part of a competitive employee-compensation package (keep in mind that all fifty states offer state government employees some type of pension plan).

The objective of any public employee compensation package should be to attract the quality and quantity of labor necessary to provide essential state and local government services to the public at the lowest cost to taxpayers. There are several economic reasons why pensions can help achieve this objective.[2]

---

1. Raquel Pichardo, "CalPERS a Model of Innovation at 75," *Pensions & Investments*, May 14, 2007.

2. This section draws from Alan Blinder's classic paper *Private Pensions and Public Pensions: Theory and Fact*, NBER Working Paper No. 902 (Cambridge, MA: National Bureau of Economic Research, 1982).

The first and most important reason is taxes. By placing a portion of total compensation into a pension fund, the worker can defer taxes. For workers far from retirement, this deferral can amount to an enormous saving because money in a pension fund accumulates at the tax-free rate of interest while savings in standard financial assets accumulate at the after-tax rate of interest. Also, when the tax is finally paid after retirement, no payroll tax is due and typically most workers will be in lower income-tax brackets than they were during their prime earnings years (this applies less, however, to California's pension millionaires).

The tax code explains why, for all practical purposes, private pensions were of minor importance in the pre–World War II era. As Princeton University Professor Alan Blinder has noted: "Except for very high income workers, the tax distortions favoring pensions over straight wages were negligible prior to World War II simply because the income tax was negligible. This is a major difference between the prewar and postwar periods, which helps explain why pensions were absent before World War II and blossomed thereafter."[3] In 1939, as Blinder noted, there were only 659 qualified private pension plans in the United States. By 1980, that number grew to 488,901 plans, according to the U.S. Department of Labor.[4] By 2010, it was 701,012.

The tax benefits of pensions help California governments attract qualified workers in competitive labor markets, wherein all fifty states offer some type of pension to state government employees. The tax advantages are especially large in California where income-tax rates are high and steeply progressive.

The second reason for pensions is that many employers want to discourage labor turnover, especially among experienced workers, because there are

1. high transaction costs to recruit and hire qualified workers;
2. cost advantages to retain current workers for whom the employer has more knowledge about their skills and abilities than prospective

---

3. Blinder, *Private Pensions,* 16.

4. U.S. Department of Labor, *Private Pension Plan Bulletin Historical Tables and Graphs* (Washington, DC: Employee Benefits Security Administration, 2012), 1.

workers outside the organization for which it might be more difficult to estimate their skills and abilities;

3. positive incentives for employers to invest in workers, teaching them skills specific to the organization, and pensions are a way to induce workers to remain with the organization long enough for it to recoup its investment costs.

Pensions also create stronger incentives for a worker to be honest or not to shirk, which is especially important if the job involves fiduciary responsibilities, because part of the worker's wages is set aside in a pension, to be paid only if the worker stays on the job long enough, and which could be forfeited in cases of malfeasance.

Blinder notes that "each of these phenomena leads to essentially the same conclusion: every worker represents a piece of (human) capital owned by the firm; if he quits, he destroys some of the firm's capital. Firms will therefore have an incentive to draw up a compensation scheme that reduces mobility; and pensions are a convenient way of doing this."[5]

The economic incentives to provide pensions are obviously greater in for-profit companies where there are "residual claimants" to any profits. But pensions also help governments retain qualified and experienced workers, encourage honesty and loyalty from employees, and promote productivity-enhancing investments in workers that yield future returns to the public. In summary, there are economic reasons why pensions can be a useful component of employee compensation packages, even in the public sector.[6]

As discussed in Chapter 5, however, there are perverse incentives for politicians to make pension benefits overly generous and to underfund them. These factors make pensions attractive to politicians for self-interested reasons, not just for the economic reasons discussed here.

---

5. Blinder, *Private Pensions*, 18.

6. Some have called for the immediate end to public employee pensions. See, for example, "Abolish California's Public Employee Pensions," *EcoWorld*, October 7, 2008.

A good steward of taxpayer money, of course, would not provide excessive pensions and would seek to make total employee compensation for a job in the public sector equal to total employee compensation for the same job in the private sector. A good steward would also choose a pension design that is efficient and effective (more on this in Chapter 8).

The next chapter presents the critical elements of a comprehensive solution to California's public pension crisis, which also could be applied anywhere in America facing a similar problem.

8

The Critical Elements of
a Comprehensive Solution

THE CONVENTIONAL APPROACH to pension reform in California has been piecemeal: small, incremental changes to many variables in existing defined-benefit plans such as changing the salary base to prevent spiking, increasing contribution rates, lengthening vesting periods, hiking the minimum retirement age, and reducing COLAs.

Politicians and government workers favor this approach because it can create the appearance of significant reform without actually doing much. It also does not threaten the status quo as much as other approaches. The California Public Employees' Pension Reform Act (PEPRA), AB 340, enacted in September 2012, is a classic example of this piecemeal approach.[1]

Although PEPRA made many changes, some of them significant reforms, most of the changes apply only to new employees because of the California Rule. The payoff in terms of savings, therefore, is backloaded and most savings will not appear for decades, *assuming the reforms are kept in place by the legislature.*

Pension changes in either direction have a slow-motion impact. As noted by John Tuohy, chairman of the pension committee of the Government Finance Officers Association: "Moving pension plans is like steering a blimp:

---

1. Government Code Sections 7522 et seq. See Office of Governor Edmund G. Brown Jr., *Governor Brown Signs Bipartisan Pension Reform Bill to Save Billions by Capping Benefits, Increasing Retirement Age, and Stopping Abuse*, News Release, September 12, 2012.

you turn the wheel and you go six miles before it starts to turn."[2] CalPERS estimated that PEPRA will save the fund between $42 billion and $55 billion over 30 years, while CalSTRS said it will save $22.7 billion over 30 years.[3] These savings might sound meaningful, but they are a drop in the bucket compared to total unfunded liabilities. The bottom line in California is that governments have few ways to control pension costs for existing workers given current law. Pay cuts and COLA reductions are the primary tools, but they have proven to be inadequate.

PEPRA is also the source of much bewilderment. Rules and regulations issued to implement and interpret PEPRA have often created more confusion than clarity. CalPERS Circular Letters web page is replete with such new rules.[4] Something as basic as what constitutes a "new employee" under PEPRA is not straightforward.

PEPRA left most of the cost drivers in place, as evidenced by growing pension debt, huge liabilities getting passed on to our children and grandchildren, government services being cut, and earned pensions in jeopardy of impairment in bankruptcy-challenged cities. By any measure, the piecemeal approach has not worked. Reforms have been inadequate. As noted by the *New York Times*: "Changes in the state employee pension system approved last year [in California] do not, in the view of most analysts, come close to addressing the long-term pension liabilities over the horizon."[5]

A comprehensive solution to California's public pension woes must do two things: (1) shore up California's current public pension plans, and (2) ensure that California never repeats this crisis. The solutions proposed here will accomplish these two goals and are also rooted in reality.

---

2. John W. Schoen, "Pandemic of Pension Woes Is Plaguing the Nation," *CNBC*, November 19, 2013.

3. Greg Risling, "California Pension Reform Bill Signed into Law by Gov. Jerry Brown," *Associated Press*, September 12, 2012.

4. See http://www.calpers.ca.gov/index.jsp?bc=/employer/cir-ltrs/home.xml.

5. Adam Nagourney, "Brown Cheered in Second Act, at Least So Far," *New York Times*, August 16, 2013.

As discussed previously, politicians in both political parties have strong, perverse incentives to mismanage defined-benefit pension plans to win votes and campaign contributions. According to Morningstar, two-thirds of state pension funds in the United States are unhealthy.[6] Public governance is generally incompatible with a responsibly run defined-benefit pension plan. California is not unique, but it nevertheless has some of the biggest problems along with Illinois and Pennsylvania. Any solution, therefore, must confront the reality of public governance head on, otherwise California is doomed to repeat the cycle of boom and bust and service insolvency.

For these reasons, increasing numbers of financial experts and political scientists are concluding that agents in the political arena cannot operate financially sustainable defined-benefit pension plans over the long haul. The incentives for political mischief are too great. For this reason alone, defined-contribution pension plans are a superior option (but more on this below).

The six recommendations offered below would fix California's public pension systems. Anything less will leave enough of the current structure in place to allow a repeat of the pension crisis in the future.

Require Financial Integrity

The *New York Times* has noted that the "politically difficult steps taken recently by many states to fix their pension problems—raising retirement ages, requiring bigger contributions from workers, lowering benefits for new hires—will prove insufficient, because they were based on underestimates of the problem."[7] This is certainly true in California.

California's pension problems will never be fixed without an honest accounting of the true size of unfunded liabilities. As long as accounting tricks can be used to hide the true scope of the problems, it is unlikely there will be sufficient political will to fix them.

---

6. Tim Reid and Lisa Lambert, "U.S. Public Pensions Need More Than Investment Windfall," *Reuters*, March 10, 2014.

7. Walsh, "Ratings Service Finds Pension Shortfall," 2013.

All California public pension funds must be required to use prudent and economically sound methods to calculate their assets and liabilities that match or exceed the standards in the private sector. This means using a risk-free government bond rate of return and real discount rate (between 3 percent and 4 percent), market value of assets, an amortization period of 15–20 years, and in most cases a minimum retirement age of 62 to begin receiving DB pension checks.

A short, prudent amortization period minimizes the intergenerational redistribution of wealth. Ventura County uses a short 15-year amortization period for its DB pension plan, proving it can be done in California.[8]

An independent panel of experts commissioned by the Society of Actuaries, an education group that also conducts the actuarial profession's licensing exams, generally supports the actuarial recommendations made here.[9]

Regarding the interest rate, the panel recommended, "the plan liability and normal cost [be] calculated at the risk-free rate" and "the rate of return assumption should be based primarily on the current risk-free rate plus explicit risk premia or on other similar forward-looking techniques." Regarding the amortization period, "amortization of gains/losses should be completed over a period of no more than 15 to 20 years." On intergenerational equity, the panel said: "Fully funding pension benefits over the average future service period of public employees reasonably aligns the cost of today's public services with the taxpayers who benefit from those services."

The blue ribbon panel of twelve academics, actuaries, and financial leaders released its recommendations in February 2014, and it calls on the separate Actuarial Standards Board to set more aggressive standards.

---

8. Anna Bitong, "Study Says Pension Reform Could Save County Millions," *Thousand Oaks (CA) Acorn,* April 17, 2014.

9. Independent Panel Commissioned by the Society of Actuaries, *Report of the Blue Ribbon Panel on Public Pension Plan Funding* (Schaumburg, IL: Society of Actuaries, February 24, 2014). The four quotes in the next paragraph of the text are from pages 7, 8, 8, and 7, respectively, of this report.

These very reasonable and responsible changes would allow the public, legislators, pension officials, and the media to know the true health of pension plans. The time is long overdue for an honest assessment. GASB's requirement that government jurisdictions report net pension liabilities on financial statements is an important step in the right direction, but more needs to be done, as described here.

Fund to the Annual Required Contribution

With transparency comes knowledge of the true scope of public pension problems. The next step is to eliminate all unfunded pension liabilities. The day of reckoning has arrived.

The California Constitution should be amended to require public pensions to fund to the annual required contribution (ARC) each year. Without this requirement, pension funds will never dig themselves out of the hole even if their actuarial assumptions prove to be 100-percent correct because, as shown previously, contributions have been consistently below the ARC. Since 1932, politicians and pension officials have declared "pension holidays" during good times, or simply failed to contribute what is needed. California should follow the lead of other states such as Oregon and enact an explicit requirement of 100-percent funding to the ARC each year.[10]

---

10. Regarding the best investment policy for ARC contributions, in a report by Donald H. Korn and colleagues at Arthur D. Little, Inc., for the Indiana Pension Management Study Commission, the report concluded:

> [T]he best investment policy of all with respect to pension *obligations* is a balanced combination of cash matching and "immunization." This means buying a portfolio of bonds that will have coupon and principal payments that match the current pension claims, and whose cash return is insensitive to changes in the level of interest rates. As the pension claims change, because of salary changes, entry and exit of personnel, and changes in the benefits, the portfolio is changed to make it immunized again. For this purpose, *only vested benefits* need to be counted. . . .
>
> From an economic point of view, a plan is fully funded when the value of the portfolio is equal to the present value of the vested benefits only, where current market interest rates are used in bringing future values to the present. If a fully funded

The first law of holes is, when you're in one, stop digging. By funding to the ARC, the pension funds would stop deficits from growing and backfill unfunded liabilities within a reasonable period of time to limit intergenerational inequities.

Fund the Annual Required Contribution without Pension Obligation Bonds

Each pension fund's ARC should be paid in full each year and any additional funds needed to do this should not come from issuing pension obligation bonds (POBs). Under the reform recommended here, the current generation pays its bills in full rather than pushing the burden onto our children and grandchildren through such risky and immoral actions as issuing pension obligation bonds.

The California Constitution should be amended to ban POBs. The idea behind POBs is that a government jurisdiction borrows money in bond markets at low interest rates and then invests that money in the higher-return pension fund, to yield a net return (after paying back the bond loan). The problem with this approach is that it seldom works for a variety of reasons.

First, the arbitrage has to be executed at just the right moment for market timing to yield a positive net return. Pension fund returns must average more than the cost of financing the debt, which is often not the case. Second, as of 1986, POBs are not exempt from federal taxation, thus their interest rate is higher than ordinary state and local bonds. Third, fees are charged by brokers

---

plan is immunized, it will remain fully funded regardless of changes in interest rates and inflation, so long as new benefits each year are funded during that year. . . .

The bonds held in the pension fund portfolio should be safe ones. Government bonds or very high grade corporate bonds would be best. Investment managers could be permitted to take more risks—for example invest in stocks—with the portion of the portfolio that does not need to be immunized.

See Donald H. Korn et al., *Study of Management and Investment Performance of the Boards of the Indiana Public Employees' Retirement Fund and the Field Examiners' Retirement Fund,* Report to the Indiana Pension Management Study Commission prepared by Arthur D. Little, Inc., January 1984.

for issuing POBs that make the arbitrage less likely to be successful. Fourth, POBs are an inflexible debt with required annual repayments unlike amortization of unfunded pension liabilities.

Alicia Munnell and colleagues analyzed all 2,931 POBs issued from 1986 through July 1, 2009.[11] They found that "by mid-2009 most POBs have been a net drain on government revenues. . . . [M]ost POBs issued since 1992 are in the red."[12] Which governments tend to issue POBs? An extensive statistical analysis by Munnell et al. concluded:

> [G]overnments are more likely to issue POBs if they are in financial stress, and already have substantial debt outstanding, and the [pension] plan represents a substantial obligation to the government. . . . [T]hose that *should not* issue a POB have done so.[13]

California governments have issued more POBs than any other state. A 2013 analysis by the Center for Investigative Reporting found that POBs for the cities of Richmond and Pasadena and the counties of Merced, San Bernardino, and San Diego have not been successful.[14] Meanwhile, in the aftermath of its 20-year pension contribution holiday, the University of California has borrowed $2.7 billion since 2011 to fund the UCRP.[15] The loans will be paid off using a special 10-year assessment on campus and medical center payrolls.

A POB is the pension sector's equivalent to a "Hail Mary" pass in football and about as successful. All told, POBs typically do not yield net positive returns; keep politicians from having to fix the underlying pension problems; and delay action, thus driving up total costs. The blue ribbon panel commissioned by the Society of Actuaries said that POBs "should not be used" and "[p]lans are not funded in a broad budgetary sense when debt is issued by the

---

11. Alicia H. Munnell et al., *Pension Obligation Bonds: Financial Crisis Exposes Risks* (Chestnut Hill, MA: Center for Retirement Research at Boston College, January 2010).

12. Munnell et al., *Pension Obligation Bonds*, 4 and 6.

13. Munnell et al., *Pension Obligation Bonds*, 6.

14. Jennifer Gollan, *California Agencies Gamble on Pension Bonds to Cover Debts—and Lose* (Sacramento: Center for Investigative Reporting, October 29, 2013).

15. Ed Mendel, "UC Borrows $2.7 Billion to Fund Pension Debt," *Calpensions.com*, July 21, 2014.

plan sponsor to fund the plan, whether inside or outside the plan."[16] California voters should ban the issuance of pension obligation bonds.[17]

In many local communities, raising taxes is not an option, so services will have to be cut further or bankruptcy declared, as has already been done in several California cities. Bankruptcy opens the door to pensioners receiving less than 100 percent of their earned DB benefits, as Detroit has proven. This is equivalent to repudiating part of the debt owned to pension creditors.[18]

If federal bankruptcy law can force reduction in all unsecured claims, including those that are fully vested in retirees under state law, then local government employees and retirees would be wise to adopt a strategy that avoids the possibility of their fully accrued benefits being put in jeopardy, which leads to the next two recommendations.

Abolish the California Rule

The policy changes discussed so far would stop past problems from getting worse. They should be adopted even if the additional recommendations to

---

16. Independent Panel, *Public Pension Plan Funding*, 31.

17. If state legislators or local politicians think new revenue is needed to fully fund pension liabilities, one approach, often overlooked, which does not involve painful tax increases, is to acquire additional revenue by selling surplus government-owned properties, and earmark the proceeds to pay pension liabilities. This approach of selling public-sector buildings and grounds has been examined thoroughly and could generate billions of dollars to backfill pension deficits. See, for example, William F. Shughart II, "Sell State Assets to Close Budget Gap," *The Press-Enterprise (Riverside, CA)*, May 8, 2008; William F. Shughart II, "Yard Sale for Cash-Strapped States," *Christian Science Monitor*, June 5, 2008; William F. Shughart II, "A Budget Solution—Sell Off San Quentin," *San Francisco Chronicle*, March 31, 2009; and William F. Shughart II, "State's Policy Is to Leave Money Sitting Idle during Deficit Times," *San Francisco Examiner*, August 6, 2009.

18. This approach is less radical than the approach favored by many libertarians: repudiate the pension debt entirely because no individual taxpayer ever made an explicit contractual agreement with an individual government employee to pay for his or her benefits. Many libertarians argue that individuals should only be required to pay for goods or services that they have voluntarily entered into a contract with another person to pay for. No such contract exists for pensions. Instead, the government entered into a "contract" for them.

follow are not adopted. But more changes must be implemented if the goal is to ensure this crisis is not repeated in the future.

The California Constitution should be amended to give state and local governments authority to modify pension benefits that current employees will earn in the future. Benefits already earned for past work performed would be unaffected. The federal government and private-sector employers have this flexibility. This change would abolish the California Rule. A constitutional amendment should state that pension benefits accrue as they are earned, but can be modified going forward. A constitutional solution would avoid significant litigation costs in the future.

Pension law scholar Amy Monahan of the University of Minnesota School of Law has argued that the case law establishing the California Rule is flawed:

[I]n holding that benefits not yet earned are contractually protected, California courts have improperly infringed on legislative power and have fashioned a rule inconsistent with both contract and economic theory.[19]

Monahan has argued that the judges created a contractual right to future accruals where one does not normally exist:

A state law does not normally create contractual rights, but "merely declares a policy to be pursued until the legislature shall ordain otherwise." . . . As the Supreme Court has explained, "to construe laws as contracts when the obligation is not clearly and unequivocally expressed would be to limit drastically the essential powers of a legislative body."[20]

Monahan concluded that "pension benefits that have already been earned through services rendered to the state should be protected against impairment, but that it is hard to find legal justification for protecting the rate of future benefit accrual."[21] Future pension benefit formulas should be seen as

---

19. Amy B. Monahan, "Statutes as Contracts? The 'California Rule' and Its Impact on Public Pension Reform," *Iowa Law Review* 97 (2012), 1029.

20. Monahan, "Statutes as Contracts?" 1037.

21. Monahan, "Statutes as Contracts?" 1079.

revocable benefits, such as Social Security benefits, not contractual rights. Once the work is performed, however, pension benefits earned become a vested right. Monahan argued elsewhere: "[S]tates would be well served to adopt a contractual approach to public pension benefits, but to limit that contractual protection to accrued benefits. This approach is clear, protects legitimate participant interests, and preserves an employer's ability to respond to changing economic conditions."[22]

The current protection of benefit formulas from the date of hire onward imposes a straightjacket on state and local governments that makes it impossible to adjust pensions going forward in the face of new financial realities. Legal scholar Richard Epstein has called this rigidity a "financial death spiral."[23]

California local governments have only three options in response to sharply rising pension costs that consume more of their budgets: raise tax rates, cut services, or declare bankruptcy. The state government cannot even declare bankruptcy. The courts' California Rule has taken the obvious move of adjusting pension benefits off the table. Simply stated, abolishing the California Rule would give government jurisdictions in California, especially local governments, the authority needed to solve their own pension problems.

Law professor Alexander Volokh agrees with this view:

> [T]he rule is unsound as a policy matter, insofar as it locks governments and public employees into compensations structures different than what they would otherwise negotiate, and makes it harder for states to reform their pension systems.[24]

Volokh has argued that pension benefits should be treated like other types of compensation: as something earned over time and not guaranteed for the future. He said:

---

22. Amy B. Monahan, "Public Pension Plan Reform: The Legal Framework," *Education, Finance, and Policy* 5 (March 2010), 1.

23. Richard A. Epstein, "Reckless Unions," *Defining Ideas*, February 17, 2014.

24. Alexander "Sasha" Volokh, *Overprotecting Public Employee Pensions: The Contract Clause and the California Rule* (Washington, DC: Federalist Society, December 2013), 4.

In addition to being more rational as a public-employee compensation policy, abandoning the California Rule would also give governmental units in California, and wherever else the rule has been adopted, flexibility to deal with changing circumstances.[25]

Likewise, former Clinton administration economic advisor Alicia Munnell and Laura Quinby, both with the Center for Retirement Research at Boston College, agree with the accrual standard that exists in sixteen states:

> In many states, a key challenge is narrowing the current definition of the employer-employee contract to establish that the contract is created when the employee performs the service. Such a standard would be much clearer than the morass of provisions that currently exists across the states, would enable state officials to undertake needed reforms, and would put public-sector workers on an even footing with those in the private sector.[26]

California's Little Hoover Commission also endorsed this change in its 2011 report:

> To provide immediate savings of the scope needed, state and local governments must have the flexibility to alter future, unaccrued retirement benefits for current workers. This notion is unpopular, but must be pursued. And it must be pursued for public safety pensions as well.
>
> Public safety personnel costs generally comprise a larger portion of government budgets than other job classifications. With higher salaries, a younger workforce, and earlier retirement ages, changes made prospectively to safety pensions for current workers help put these plans on a sustainable footing more quickly.[27]

---

25. Volokh, *Overprotecting Public Employee Pensions*, 19.

26. Alicia H. Munnell and Laura Quinby, *Legal Constraints on Changes in State and Local Pensions*, State and Local Pension Plans Report Number 25 (Chestnut Hill, MA: Center for Retirement Research at Boston College, August 2012), 4.

27. Little Hoover, *Public Pensions*, 42–43.

The University of California has even boldly declared that it reserves "the right to change UCRP benefit provisions prospectively for both current and future employees. These changes would not apply to the benefits that have been accrued by current employees prior to the effective date of the changes."[28] This standard should operate across all California government agencies.

In early October 2014, Judge Christopher M. Klein of the U.S. Bankruptcy Court, Eastern District of California, ruled that the city of Stockton may legally cut already-promised pension payments and walk away from its CalPERS contract as part of a bankruptcy restructuring plan. For the first time, a judge in California said a local government has the right to reject its contract with CalPERS in bankruptcy. Klein stated: "impairing contractual obligations—that's what bankruptcy's all about"[29] and ruled that state law protecting pensions takes a back seat to the federal bankruptcy code and the U.S. Constitution, otherwise, "the California legislature can edit the federal law."[30] Even though Stockton's final restructuring plan did not cut pensions, Klein's groundbreaking decision stands, making this a possible avenue for trimming the pensions of current retirees and employees of bankrupt local governments in California. Public pensions are no longer sacrosanct.

Switch to Reasonably Priced Defined-Contribution Pension Plans

Abolishing the California Rule would allow for flexibility on how public pensions are structured going forward for all employees. It would give state and local governments the tools they need to fix California's pension plans.

---

28. University of California, "Q&A: Are the Regents Allowed to Change the Pension Plan (Not Retiree Health Benefits) Now Covering Current Employees, or Only for Future Employees?" August 19, 2010.

29. Steven Greenhut, "Bankruptcy Ruling Not As Bad As It Looks," *U-T San Diego*, October 31, 2014.

30. Mary Williams Walsh, "Bankruptcy Judge in California Challenges Sanctity of Pensions," *New York Times*, October 1, 2014.

But what is the best pension structure? One need only look to the more competitive private sector for the answer.

As it stands, the state government and many local governments have made promises to workers they cannot afford. For those California state and local governments that want a more responsible and sustainable approach to employee pensions, one approach is to vest all accrued pension benefits as of a certain date and then switch to a reasonably priced 401(k)–style defined-contribution pension plan for all new hires and current public employees going forward. Alaska and Michigan have switched completely to a mandatory DC retirement plan for state employees.[31] This approach allows each government jurisdiction to decide whether to switch to a DC plan; but if a switch occurs, it is best for it to apply to all employees, including teachers and public safety workers. There should be no sacred cows.

Since the state of California is not the employer of California's public school teachers, the districts themselves should be responsible for paying DC contributions for teachers. Governor Brown has hinted that he also supports relieving the state of future contributions to CalSTRS. The governor's proposed budget in January 2014 said: "Because retirement costs are part of total compensation costs, school districts and community colleges should anticipate absorbing much of any new CalSTRS funding requirement. The state's long-term role as a direct contributor to the plan should be evaluated."[32] The LAO also supports "an end to direct state payments to the [CalSTRS] system a few decades from now—once today's unfunded liabilities are fully paid off."[33]

---

31. Pension Review Board, *A Review of Defined Benefit, Defined Contribution, and Alternative Retirement Plans*, Research Paper No. 12–001 (Austin, TX: Pension Review Board, May 2012), 38; and Adam B. Summers, *How California's Public Pension System Broke (and How to Fix It)*, Policy Study 382 (Los Angeles: Reason Foundation, June 2010), 27.

32. John Fensterwald, "Brown Projects Big Increase in School Spending in Next State Budget," *EdSource*, January 9, 2014.

33. Ryan Miller and Jason Sisney, *Perspectives on the CalSTRS Funding Scenarios Discussed at the March 19, 2014, Joint Hearing* (Sacramento: Legislative Analyst's Office, March 19, 2014), 4.

Ideally, the state constitution should be amended to prohibit awarding retroactive pension benefits or awarding retroactive increases to pension benefits. All benefits should be go-forward for work completed in the future.

A recent statewide poll by the Public Policy Institute of California found that 73 percent of likely voters in California favor changing the pension system for new public employees to a 401(k)–style defined-contribution system.[34] In other words, there is widespread public support for greater use of DC retirement plans for public employees in California. The public is ahead of politicians on this issue.

Butrica et al. have noted that this transition has been happening for some time in the private sector:

> More recently, many employers have frozen their DB plans. . . . Some experts expect that most private-sector plans will be frozen in the next few years and eventually terminated. . . . Under the typical DB plan freeze, current participants will receive retirement benefits based on their accruals up to the date of the freeze, but will not accumulate any additional benefits; new employees will not be covered. Instead, employers will either establish new DC plans or increase contributions to existing DC plans.[35]

Ideally, this is the approach that California governments should take by establishing a date of record, vest DB pensions accrued for work completed, close the DB plans, and open new DC plans. DB plans and hybrid plans leave the door open for vote buying through political manipulation of pension plans. Long-term, it is best to terminate the DB plans.

There are different ways to structure DC plans, including individual plans and pooled plans, but regardless of the structure, government contributions to

---

34. Baldassare et al., *Californians and Their Government,* 16.
35. Butrica et al., *Disappearing Defined Benefit Pension.*

DC plans should be mandatory each month or each pay period just as paying wages and salaries is required.[36]

Michigan established its DC plan in 1997 owing to concerns about cost unpredictability in its DB plan.[37] All Michigan state employees participate in Social Security. Government employers make a mandatory contribution of 4 percent of salary into each employee's personal DC account, plus offer an employee match up to 3 percent. Employees are not required to contribute, but must contribute 3 percent to receive the maximum state match of 3 percent. Full vesting occurs after 4 years' employment.

Alaska established its DC plan in 2006 owing to concerns over growing unfunded liabilities in its DB plan.[38] Alaska's plan covers state employees and teachers, neither of whom participate in Social Security. Government employers contribute 9.57 percent for general civilian employees, 10.32 percent for public safety employees, and 11.61 percent for teachers. All employees contribute 8 percent. Full vesting occurs after 5 years' employment.

---

36. Some concerns regarding defined-contribution pension plans have been raised in the law and economics literature. For example, Professor Jack Beermann has argued, "defined contribution plans have problems of their own, mainly due to faulty design. According to Professor [Paul] Secunda, many employees in voluntary defined contribution plans tend not to save enough and do not have adequate information or knowledge to direct their investments. These problems could easily be resolved through better plan design." See Jack M. Beermann, "Essay: Resolving the Public Pension 'Crisis,'" *Fordham Urban Law Journal* (forthcoming 2014), 12. Some of the variables that must be defined for each plan are the contribution rates, vesting period, universe of investment options, and the default participation rules. One proposed system of default rules is (1) automatic enrollment of employees in the DC plan with an opt-out option; (2) index funds as the default investment option; (3) target-date adjustments as the default so the asset mix automatically changes according to an employee's lifecycle—aggressive portfolios for younger workers and more conservative for older workers (again, with an opt-out option); and (4) an option for employees' to convert their DC account balances into an annuity at retirement. See Truong Bui, "How to Structure a Good Defined Contribution Plan," *Out of Control Policy Blog*, Reason Foundation, July 22, 2014.

37. For a summary of Michigan's plans, see Pension Review Board, *Review of Defined Benefit*, 21–22.

38. For a summary of Alaska's plans, see Pension Review Board, *Review of Defined Benefit*, 23–24.

A framework for a 401(k)–style DC plan has been developed for Ventura County, California, by the Ventura County Taxpayers Association. The *Sustainable Retirement System Initiative* is modeled after a successful 2012 initiative in San Diego.[39] Under this proposal, the government's mandatory contributions to new employee retirement accounts would be limited to

- 4 percent of employee compensation to non-public-safety employees who are enrolled in Social Security;
- 11 percent of employee compensation to public-safety employees not enrolled in Social Security;
- 5 percent of employee compensation to public-safety employees who are enrolled in Social Security.

The Ventura County proposal would not require a matching contribution from employees.

Switching to a reasonably priced defined-contribution plan of between 4 percent and 10 percent of payroll would yield significant cost savings. Annual payments to defined-benefit public pension plans in California typically range from 20 percent to 35 percent of payroll, but has been even higher in some cases.[40]

The closure of the DB plans raises the question of "employee reliance interest": Is it fair to close DB plans that current employees expected to be in place for the reminder of their public-sector tenure and have made plans based on this expectation? It could be argued that the employees' reliance on this expectation caused them to turn down better-paying jobs in the private sector or caused them to make purchases assuming a total future pension benefit. Shouldn't an exception be made for current employees, allowing them to continue in the DB plan until their retirement rather than switching all employees to a DC plan?

---

39. See http://committeeforpensionfairness.org/about-the-initiative.html.
40. Danny Brown et al., *General Session: Pension Reform*, 2012 CalPERS Educational Forum.

First, it is important to emphasize that under the reform plan presented here all accrued pension benefits will be paid in full. If a current employee has worked 15 years for a government agency, they will receive a defined benefit pension based on 15 years of service. There is very little employee reliance interest, therefore, for public employees near retirement and for those very early in their careers—it is most relevant to employees in the middle of their careers.

Second, employee reliance interest resides in contract law ("expectation, reliance, and restitution"). If there is a true, formal employment contract in place, then that contract should be honored until it expires.

Third, once a contract expires, or for those at-will employees with no contract, then as argued earlier, pension benefits should vest at the time that work is completed. Going forward, changes to pension benefit accruals should be permitted. Current employees, however, can ask for higher straight pay as compensation for the lower DC pension benefits in the future. Clearly, there is some level of straight pay that would compensate them for any pension losses. If that pay level is higher than what elected officials, government agencies, taxpayers, and voters are willing to pay, current employees are free to accept better offers in the private sector. As stated earlier, the objective of any public employee compensation package should be to attract the quality and quantity of labor necessary to provide essential state and local government services to the public at the lowest cost to taxpayers. The objective is not to create pension millionaires.

The closure of DB plans ensures that this crisis will never happen again and it essentially caps the pension debt as just another form of debt that must be paid in order to fulfill obligations for past work performed.[41] Josh McGee,

---

41. Richard Riordan and Tim Rutten have proposed a plan that would allow local, and perhaps state, governments to sell long-term bonds to cover their pension liabilities, with the federal government guaranteeing repayment using funds accumulated from fees paid by participants. Riordan and Rutten claim there would be "no net cost to Washington." In exchange for the federal bond insurance, and to curb a "moral hazard" that pension benefits will be increased and contributions cut knowing the federal government will guarantee bond repayment, the participants would agree to certain reforms such as "negotiated reductions in current benefits." See Riordan and Rutten, "A Plan to Avert the Pension Crisis."

vice president of public accountability at the Laura and John Arnold Foundation, has noted:

> Paying the pension debt is the sole responsibility of the public employers who participate in the plan. . . . Moving new workers to a new system does not affect the funded level of past benefit accruals, nor does it affect the debt service payments employers must make to pay off any accrued debt. The pension debt is a bill that is owed to public workers for past service, and this debt must be paid regardless of the go-forward retirement savings system.[42]

A prudent pension debt payment schedule should be established, one that limits intergenerational shifting of the burden, and it should be adhered to just like any bond payment schedule. As noted by Robert Costrell, professor of economics at the University of Arkansas:

> The decision on scheduling amortization payments on the unfunded accrued liability (UAL) is a financial policy decision, not much different from the decision on scheduling debt service payments on ordinary debt. How to structure future benefits is a separate policy decision. Pension reform proposals should be evaluated on their own merits and not confused with amortization schedules. Amortization pays for past debts; pension reform lays a path toward a responsible future.[43]

A 15-year, level-dollar amortization schedule will pay off the pension debt faster; save taxpayer's money long-term; pay off debt when it is due, that is, when workers retire; and reduces the "cost to carry," thereby cutting the overall cost of the pension debt service. "Transition-cost" arguments against switching to DC plans are myths.[44]

---

42. Josh B. McGee, *The Transition Cost Mirage—False Arguments Distract from Real Pension Reform Debates*, LJAF Policy Perspective (Houston: Laura and John Arnold Foundation, March 2013), 7.

43. Robert M. Costrell, *"GASB Won't Let Me"—A False Objection to Public Pension Reform*, LJAF Policy Perspective (Houston: Laura and John Arnold Foundation, May 2012), 4.

44. For more on this see McGee, *Transition Cost Mirage*; and Costrell, *GASB Won't Let Me*.

Require Voter Approval

Charter cities in California that operate independent pension systems, for example, Los Angeles, San Francisco, and Fresno, require voter approval of pension changes. The California Constitution should be amended to require voter preapproval of any change to a state or local pension plan that increases taxpayer financial obligations, including initial and subsequent defined-contribution rates. This will prevent politicians from foisting further pension burdens on taxpayers without their explicit consent. The Little Hoover Commission noted:

> Requiring a public vote on pension increases also would provide an additional safeguard for taxpayers. Public votes do not necessarily block pension increases; they put a higher burden on employees to make the case for the enhancement. Cities with pension formulas etched into charters, such as San Francisco, already put proposed public pension increases before voters. . . . A rash of local initiatives in November 2010 that supported the process for voter-approved pension increases speaks to the public demand for this level of oversight.[45]

San Francisco's requirement has enabled the city to avoid some of the pension problems visited on other California cities over the years.[46]

What Is Old Is New Again

In 1978, the Democratic-controlled U.S. House of Representatives released an 858-page report on federal, state, and local government pension systems.[47] The investigation was conducted by the Committee on Education and Labor

---

45. Little Hoover, *Public Pensions*, 52.

46. George Passantino, "San Diego Pension Proposals Don't Do Enough," *San Diego Union-Tribune*, August 23, 2005.

47. Committee on Education and Labor, U.S. House of Representatives, *Pension Task Force Report on Public Employee Retirement Systems*, 95th Congress, 2nd Session (Washington, DC: U.S. Government Printing Office, March 15, 1978).

chaired by Representative Carl Perkins (D-Kentucky). Among other key findings, the report concluded:[48]

- Serious deficiencies exist among public employee retirement systems at all levels of government regarding the extent to which important information is reported and disclosed to plan participants, public officials, and taxpayers
- Public employee retirement systems at all levels of government are not operated in accordance with the generally accepted financial and accounting procedures applicable to private pension plans and other important financial enterprises
- There is an incomplete assessment of true pension costs at all levels of government due to the lack of adequate actuarial valuations and standards. . . . In the vast majority of public employee retirement systems, plan participants, plan sponsors, and the general public are kept in the dark with regard to a realistic assessment of true pension costs. The high degree of pension cost blindness which pervades the PERS is due to the lack of actuarial valuations, the use of unrealistic actuarial assumptions, and the general absence of actuarial standards

These conclusions from the 1978 Perkins report could have been written in 2015 about California's public pension plans and those in other states. All of these issues are addressed by the reforms recommended here.

There are many advantages to the comprehensive solutions presented here, which will be discussed in the next chapter. But some of the primary advantages are that governments must make good on pensions earned for work already performed, but, in exchange, governments are required to be financially transparent and are given the authority to switch to affordable pension plans that better protect core service levels, past and future pension benefits, taxpayer interests, and responsible budgeting.

---

48. Committee on Education and Labor, U.S. House of Representatives, *Pension Task Force Report,* "Committee Findings and Conclusions," 3 and 4.

California's public pension systems are asking for one of the biggest taxpayer bailouts in U.S. history. In exchange for billions in public assistance and public sacrifice, changes should be adopted that prevent this crisis from ever being repeated. This is fair.

The next chapter emphasizes that it is in the interests of public employees, retirees, and people who value traditional government services to accept these pension changes, even if they might disagree with them at some level.

How a Comprehensive Public Pension Solution Benefits You

THE REFORMS PRESENTED in Chapter 8 would stop the bleeding and provide a sustainable path going forward. Next, Section III explains the fiscal and moral advantages of the recommended approach.

Chapter 9 details the fiscal benefits for consumers of government services, public employees and retirees, taxpayers, voters, legislators, younger people, and poorer people. It argues that current and future government retirees, in particular, would be wise to accept the recommended reforms because they would fully pay for accrued benefits and decouple future retirement benefits from government treasuries, which are increasingly teetering on bankruptcy or already insolvent.

In addition to being the fiscally sound approach, the comprehensive solution is also the moral approach. Chapter 10 details the moral advantages of the reform recommendations, specifically that the reforms would fully fund benefits already earned, make public-sector pensions comparable to private-sector pensions, and establish intergenerational equity by stopping the redistribution of wealth from future generations to the current generation through pension funding. The methods and arguments presented here are applicable to any pension reform effort in America.

9

The Fiscal Advantages

Benefits to Consumers of Government Services

THE PENSION REFORMS recommended in Chapter 8 would create more room in budgets to provide traditional government services, if desired by the people.

Better Protect Traditional Local Government Services

At the local level, the costs of providing public pensions are growing faster than other categories of spending. Pension costs are consuming an ever-larger share of local budgets, squeezing out traditional services that past generations have counted on and enjoyed, such as effective classroom instruction, open public libraries, clean parks, and safe streets.

Figure 9.1 shows the average annual growth rate of pension costs from 1999 through 2011 in California's local independent public pension systems. In Orange County, pension costs have increased more than 31 percent *each year.* Even the lowest growth rate of 9.5 percent in Los Angeles County means that pension costs will double every 7.5 years. These staggering growth rates mean that local budgets are being consumed by ever-larger pension costs, leaving less for other services.

Figure 9.2 shows pension costs as a share of total city or county budgets. In many cases, the share is already approaching Professor Joshua Rauh's benchmark of 20 percent, which has triggered significant pension reform or

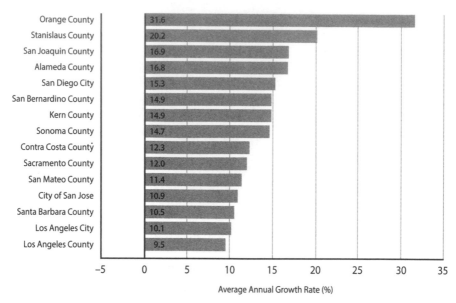

Source: Evan Storms and Joe Nation, *More Pension Math: Funded Status, Benefits, and Spending Trends for California's Largest Independent Public Employee Pension Systems* (Stanford: Stanford Institute for Economic Policy Research, February 21, 2012), 16.

Figure 9.1. Explosive growth of pension costs in California's local independent public employee pension systems, average annual growth rates 1999–2011

bankruptcy in other jurisdictions. For example, Ventura County contributes 17 percent of its budget to the pension fund. Its contributions have gone from $45 million in 2004 to $162 million in 2013, a 260-percent increase in just 9 years.[1] Pension contributions will balloon to $226 million in five years. The county's unfunded pension liability is $953 million, assuming it earns 7.75 percent per year forever on its investments. In the past five years, the pension fund has earned only 5.8 percent. The pension deficit has increased to this level from $290 million just five years ago. Using a more appropriate discount rate of 3.9 percent, Ventura County's unfunded pension liability explodes to $3.7 billion.[2]

---

1. Bitong, "Taxpayer Group Trying."

2. Ed Ring, "The Financial Impact of Pension Obligations on Ventura County," *Union-Watch,* June 24, 2014.

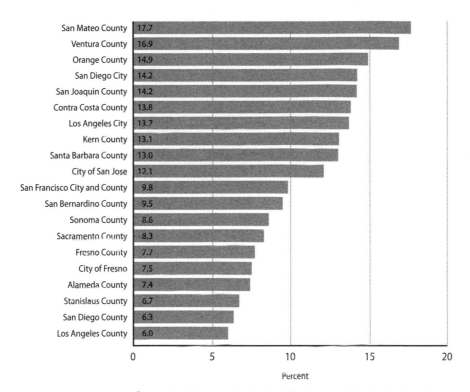

San Mateo County — 17.7
Ventura County — 16.9
Orange County — 14.9
San Diego City — 14.2
San Joaquin County — 14.2
Contra Costa County — 13.8
Los Angeles City — 13.7
Kern County — 13.1
Santa Barbara County — 13.0
City of San Jose — 12.1
San Francisco City and County — 9.8
San Bernardino County — 9.5
Sonoma County — 8.6
Sacramento County — 8.3
Fresno County — 7.7
City of Fresno — 7.5
Alameda County — 7.4
Stanislaus County — 6.7
San Diego County — 6.3
Los Angeles County — 6.0

Percent

Source: Evan Storms and Joe Nation, *More Pension Math: Funded Status, Benefits, and Spending Trends for California's Largest Independent Public Employee Pension Systems* (Stanford: Stanford Institute for Economic Policy Research, February 21, 2012), 16.

Figure 9.2. Share of local budgets devoted to pension costs associated with California's local independent public employee pension systems, 2011

As an example of the savings from switching new hires to a DC plan, which is all that can be currently implemented given the California Rule, the Reason Foundation conducted an independent actuarial analysis of the proposed ballot initiative to reform the Ventura County Employees' Retirement Association (VCERA). The actuary, William J. Sheffler, concluded that the county would save $460 million in cash over 15 years (2017–31). Cumulative cash savings would equal $5.4 million in the first 2 years alone and nearly $52 million over the first 5 years. The reforms would also reduce VCERA's liabilities by nearly $1.8 billion from 2016–31, as the county's DB plan would wind down over time.[3]

In other jurisdictions, even though a pension share of the budget might be low now, its growth rate might be high; meaning that a greater percentage of the budget will be devoted to pension costs going forward. Alameda County and Stanislaus County fit this description.

Overall, pension costs as a share of local budgets were, on average, *five times* higher in 2011 than in 1999.[4] Reducing pension shares by freezing DB plans and switching to DC plans will free room in budgets for other services.

Better Protect Traditional State Government Services

At the state level, the share of California's general fund budget devoted to pensions and retiree healthcare benefits have doubled over the past 10 years.[5] Table 9.1 shows that members, employers, and the state government contributed $19.222 billion in fiscal year 2013 to the Big Three pension systems, but it will climb to at least $20.422 billion when CalPERS's new longevity contribution fully kicks-in to account for retirees' longer lifespans.

Keep in mind that the contributions listed in Table 9.1 are made pursuant to the flawed actuarial methodology used by the pension systems. The correct approach would require even larger contributions to make the funds solvent. For example, if CalSTRS's funding is calculated using evaluation formulas and unfunded liability payback terms recommended by Moody's Investor Services, the contribution must increase to $15.4 billion a year—an increase of more than 2.5 times.[6] This calculation is based on a level payment, 20-year

---

3. Anthony Randazzo, *Ventura County Pension Reform Would Save $460 Million, Reduce Debt $1.8 Billion*, Reason Foundation Pension Reform Actuarial Analysis, Policy Brief 121 (Los Angeles: Reason Foundation, May 2014).

4. Storms and Nation, *More Pension Math*, 15.

5. "Who Pays the Bill?" *The Economist*, July 27–August 2, 2013, 26.

6. Ed Ring, *Are Annual Contributions into CalSTRS Adequate?* (Tustin: California Public Policy Center, November 8, 2013).

Table 9.1. Contributions to California's Big Three pension systems, 2013 (billions of dollars)

	Members' Contribution	Employers' Contribution	State Contribution	New State Longevity Contribution	Total
CalPERS	3.896	8.124	3.5 of the 8.124	1.2	13.220
CalSTRS	2.337	2.283	1.328	N/A	5.948
UCRP	0.416	0.810	0.028	N/A	1.254
Total	6.649	7.717	4.856	1.2	20.422

Sources: California Public Employees' Retirement System, *Comprehensive Annual Financial Report: Fiscal Year Ended June 30, 2013* (Sacramento: CalPERS, January 2014), 42; California State Teachers' Retirement System, *CalSTRS Comprehensive Annual Financial Report 2013* (West Sacramento: CalSTRS, 2014), 46; and University of California, *Retirement System 2012–2013 Annual Financial Report* (Oakland: University of California Office of the President, October 9, 2013), 18 and 51.

amortization, and 6.2 percent rate-of-return projection. A lower rate of return would increase the required contribution even more.

Regardless, $19–20 billion of taxpayer money is pouring into the Big Three pension funds each year, and more will have to be contributed if these DB plans are closed and debts paid off soon, as recommended in Chapter 8. At a minimum, roughly $6 billion more must be contributed each year to pay down the unfunded liabilities over about 30 years. This figure assumes the pension funds will hit their targeted actuarial assumptions. CalPERS claims it is providing at least 100 percent of its ARC now, so CalPERS would not have to contribute more than it has currently scheduled in order to pay off its unfunded liability in 30 years.[7] CalSTRS needs about $5 billion more each year for 32 years to pay off its unfunded liability.[8] That is about $800 per student each year that will go to pension costs, not school buildings or

---

7. California Public Employees' Retirement System, *Comprehensive Annual Financial Report: Fiscal Year Ended June 30, 2013* (Sacramento: CalPERS, January 2014), 85.

8. This will result from AB 1469 enacted in June 2014. See "Governor Signs Bill to Fix CalSTRS Funding Deficit," Association of California School Administrators, June 30, 2014.

classroom instruction. And UCRP needs about $1 billion more each year to eliminate its unfunded liability in 30 years.[9]

If the pension funds do not meet their actuarial assumptions, more money will have to be contributed each year. David Crane has estimated that paying off the true unfunded liability over 30 years would require $12–18 billion per year and $19–28 billion per year if paid off over 15 years.[10]

Today the equivalent of 18 percent of the state's general fund budget is being contributed to the Big Three pension funds each year ($19.222 billion divided by $108 billion). Under the best-case scenario of a $6 billion annual increase, this share would jump to roughly 25 percent. If assumptions are not met, contributions would easily exceed 30 percent of the budget.

Pension costs are consuming an ever-larger share of the California state budget, and more will be consumed going forward. This money is being taken from discretionary programs that many Californians value, such as the University of California, California State University, health, welfare, and the environment. But by freezing the DB plans, capping their debt, and switching to reasonably-priced DC plans, the state would save billions of dollars a year that could be used to help pay off the unfunded liability of the old DB plans and ultimately restore public services. State employees would then receive pension benefits more in line with those offered in the private sector, and public services would be better protected.

The reality is that California residents are reaching the point where they refuse to increase taxes on themselves. In response, local officials have cut services and some have filed for bankruptcy protection. Bankruptcy is not an option for the state government, however, so it has had to cut services, particularly education spending, infrastructure maintenance, and social ser-

---

9. This was calculated by taking UCRP's covered payroll of $8.6 billion and multiplying it by 11.55 percent, the employer's unfunded actuarial accrued liability payroll rate. See Segal Company, *Annual Actuarial Valuations for the University of California Retirement Plan and Its Segments and for the 1991 University of California Public Employees' Retirement System Voluntary Early Retirement Incentive Program*, November 14, 2013, 6.

10. David Crane, "California: The Trouble With Kicking the Can Down the Road," *Huffington Post*, July 14, 2009.

vices. The California Rule takes off the table the direct approach of adjusting pensions for current employees.

This is why current DB pensions are unsustainable. Raising taxes enough to make DB plans solvent is impossible politically, which results in financially unsustainable pension systems given current benefit levels, contribution rates, investment performance, and legal constraints. Injecting $6 billion more into state pensions through tax increases alone would require yet *another* Proposition 30–sized tax increase, an unlikely scenario given how narrowly Prop. 30 passed in 2012. Unless California residents want to see classrooms starved, bridges fall, roads crumble, or more local-government bankruptcies, they should support the pension reforms presented in Chapter 8.

And if federal bankruptcy law can force cuts in all unsecured claims, including those that are fully vested in retirees under state law, then local government employees and retirees would be wise to adopt a strategy that avoids the possibility of their fully accrued benefits being put in jeopardy.

Such a strategy is accepting the reforms presented in Chapter 8 because these reforms will more quickly pay off pension debts associated with accrued benefits that will be honored fully for current and future retirees.

Freezing the DB plans and switching to DC plans will save money long-term for traditional state and local services, such as education, police and fire protection, libraries, and roads and bridges. Without pension reform, inadequate investment in infrastructure will continue—California already has a deferred maintenance bill of nearly $65 billion.[11]

A full actuarial analysis of the potential savings from the recommended reforms is beyond the scope of this book. But a preliminary analysis reveals that long-term savings would be substantial. As shown in Table 9.2, total annual normal cost payments to the Big Three exceeds $14 billion per year. These payments would cease once the DB plans are closed. The annual cost of funding a reasonably-priced DC plan would be about $8 billion under the

---

11. Lawrence J. McQuillan, "California's Immoral Mountain of Debt," *The Beacon*, February 3, 2014.

Table 9.2. The contribution breakdown for the Big Three pension funds, 2013 (billions of dollars)

	CalPERS	CalSTRS	UCRP
Total taxpayer contributions[1]	12.02 (13.22 with longevity increase)	5.948	1.254
Normal cost payments (normal cost rate × covered payroll)	8.17	4.703	1.254
Normal cost rate (%)	19.0[2]	18.259[3]	15.0[4]
Covered payroll[5]	43.0	25.759	8.6
Unfunded liability payments (total contributions minus normal cost)	3.85	1.245	0.0
Employer's Unfunded Actuarial Accrued Liability (UAAL) rate (%)	6.2[2]	24.2[3]	11.55[6]

Total annual normal cost payments = 14.127

Sources:
1. See Table 9.1
2. Center for Retirement Research at Boston College, *The State of California Summary: California Pension Plans*, February 2013, 3
3. Milliman, *Defined Benefit Program Actuarial Valuation as of June 30, 2013* (Seattle: Milliman, March 20, 2014), 15
4. University of California Board of Regents, "Regents Approve Increased Pension Contributions for 2013," November 28, 2011
5. See each fund's comprehensive annual financial report, 2013, listed in Table 9.1
6. See footnote 9

assumptions that no California state employees participate in Social Security and the DC rate equals the highest rate used in Michigan or Alaska, which is roughly 10 percent of payroll. Both these assumptions are extremely cautious. The DC contribution amount is the result of multiplying total covered payroll of $77.4 billion by 10 percent.

By freezing the DB plans and switching to DC plans, California could save at least $6 billion a year ($14 billion minus $8 billion), which would fully pay for the DB closure costs discussed earlier if the government's actuarial scenario proves to be correct. Depending on how reality compares to the assumptions, however, more money might be needed each year to pay off the old DB pension debt—two or three times more if Crane is correct—which would then require additional service reductions, tax increases, or the less painful option of selling government property.

Nevertheless, $6 billion per year would make a significant contribution toward paying down past pension debt (in other words paying for all earned pension benefits) while capping the debt, limiting the intergenerational transfer of debt burdens, better protecting public services, and providing pension benefits going forward that are competitive with those offered in the private sector. Once the pension debt is paid, the tremendous savings could be redirected to restoring public services or refunded to taxpayers. Without the reforms recommended in Chapter 8, however, pension burdens will be crushing, growing, and repeatable.

California residents who value the continued provision of traditional government services should support the reforms in Chapter 8.

Benefits to Current and Future
Public Employees and Retirees

Switching from a system of DB pensions to DC pensions shifts some risks from taxpayers to individual participants. For example, under a DC plan, the individual assumes the risk of poor investment returns, the risk that they might outlive their assets, and the risk that inflation will erode the value of their nest egg in retirement, whereas DB plans provide a fixed monthly payment for life and typically with annual COLAs. These risks are transferred from taxpayers to individuals in DC pension plans. The riskier and typically less-generous structure of DC plans, however, is offset by the reduced supply of workers seeking jobs with DC benefits and consequently higher wages, everything else the same.

Notwithstanding risk-shifting effects, switching from a system of DB pensions to DC pensions has several advantages for public employees.

Ownership and Portability of Retirement Assets

With a DC plan, individual workers own their retirement accounts. They will be able to bequeath the funds to heirs upon death—forbidden under current DB systems. And since the employee owns the account, it is completely portable after vesting, meaning that if the employee leaves the public sector, the DC plan can be taken with them. Employees are not slaves to their pensions. They keep what they have earned and can take it with them.

With more control under DC plans, employees can choose an investment portfolio that better matches their individual risk preference. A relatively wealthy employee, for example, might want to gamble more than the DB plan allows.

At the local level, Detroit demonstrates that in bankruptcy, pensioners might be judged to be another class of unsecured creditors and pension benefits could be subject to full or partial impairment. If this becomes the law in California in the wake of the Stockton decision, pensioners would see DC plans as a safer alternative to DB plans. Under a DC plan, benefits are not put at risk by being tied to the financial health of the municipal government. And with a greater likelihood of responsible funding, DC plans provide public-sector employees with increased security. Many employees would prefer a system where their retirement funds are not tied long-term to the health of the local public treasury. Randall Holcombe, professor of economics at Florida State University, has put it in stark terms:

> [T]he future is here, and the retirees who bargained for pensions in excess of government's ability to pay them are finding out that those defined benefit pensions may not have been such a good bargain after all.

Defined contribution pensions are a fiscally responsible way for governments to run their pension plans. It is now becoming apparent that they are also better for the government workers who will draw them.[12]

Higher Rates of Return for Younger and Shorter-Term Workers

The current system locks employees into a rigid benefit calculation that deprives some workers of achieving greater investment gains. Anthony Archie and Peter Ferrara have analyzed the disparate impact of California's DB system on younger and shorter-term employees versus older and longer-term workers.[13]

Switching from DB plans to DC plans will typically benefit younger workers the most as well as those who stay with the government for a shorter time. Because the California DB system bases its benefits on age, years of service, and peak salary, it favors older, longer-term workers. Archie and Ferrara explained:

Say a worker, Linda, enters government employment at age 22 and continues to work for the state for 15 years. At age 37, Linda then leaves for a private-sector job. Although Linda will obtain a small government pension upon her retirement years later, the final salary used to calculate her benefits at retirement will be the salary she earned at age 37, her last year of public employment. No salary increases for the next 25–30 years of Linda's career will be counted.

By contrast, suppose another worker, Max, starts employment at 22, continues working for the same government employer for 40 years, and retires at 62. As compared to Linda, Max's benefits will naturally equal

---

12. Randall Holcombe, "Defined Benefit or Defined Contribution? Which Is the Better Way to Structure Government Pensions?" *The Beacon*, August 6, 2013.

13. Anthony P. Archie and Peter J. Ferrara, *Pension Intervention: Reforming California's Public Employee Retirement Systems* (Sacramento: Pacific Research Institute, February 2006).

an additional two percent of salary for each additional year worked past age 37, which fairly gives him credit for the additional years worked. But this additional two percent per year will be taken against the final salary at age 62, which will include 25 years of additional salary increases. This gives Max more benefits for each year of work than Linda.

To make matters worse, the contributions paid into the system for Linda by the state agency during her years of employment continued to earn investment returns for many years after she left public employment. Because she left early, Linda will get nothing for all the years of investment returns gained from the employer contributions made on her behalf. . . . [T]hese returns will be redistributed to finance the higher benefits of the workers like Max.

Inflation makes the problem even worse. As a public employee, Max received annual cost of living adjustments. This greatly influenced his final benefit calculation since it boosted his salary figure. For Linda, this inflation compensation stopped when she left government employment. The figure used to calculate Linda's benefit calculation is her salary at age 37 without any cost of living increase. Thus, the value of her benefits will consequently be depreciated by inflation because the salary figure had been depreciated by inflation over the years.[14]

Archie and Ferrara calculated the benefits that the current CalPERS plan would provide to certain hypothetical workers compared to what Governor Schwarzenegger's 2005 defined-contribution plan would have provided. They found that workers who left public employment before retirement after 10, 15, and 20 years of service would have done substantially better under a DC plan:

Currently, there are 160,000 state employees under the age of 50. Given that three out of every four employees leave public employment before retirement and that job tenure among workers under 50 is low, we found that a defined contribution pension plan would be a better

---

14. Archie and Ferrara, *Pension Intervention,* 25–26.

deal for those 120,000 employees under age 50 who choose to leave the public sector.[15]

Stops Intergenerational Redistribution of Wealth

With people living longer on average, the extended lifespan means additional years of retirement benefits. With a substantial cohort of government employees soon to retire,[16] DB contribution rates are being increased to meet the obligations to soon-to-be retirees. This negatively impacts younger workers in DB plans the most because they are forced to pay for their predecessor's retirement. For example, as noted previously, the 20-year plan to pay off CalSTRS's debt includes a $7.5 billion intergenerational redistribution.

In a DC plan, all contributions go directly into an individual's personal retirement account. If DC contributions are increased, the added contributions only add more money to that employee's account.

Ensures Pension Benefits Already Earned Are Paid

Given the amount of pension debt in California, current and future retirees at the local-government level could risk pension cuts in bankruptcy if they do not accept changes today. The recommended reforms in Chapter 8 ensure that benefits earned for work already performed are paid in full in exchange for freezing DB plans and switching to DC plans going forward.

This approach protects accrued benefits for current and future retirees, which is ultimately in the best interest of pension participants, relative to a system that cannot meet its financial obligations. Many current and retired public employees would prefer a system that freezes DB plans if it means guaranteeing that their earned DB benefits are fully paid. Budget savings from the

---

15. Archie and Ferrara, *Pension Intervention,* 27.

16. The California State Personnel Board estimates that the number of employees age 50 and beyond will increase in the next five to seven years. Nearly two thirds of California's workforce is composed of those who are baby boomers or older. See Archie and Ferrara, *Pension Intervention,* 24.

shift to DC plans can help pay for the accrued DB benefits or expand employment opportunities, especially for police officers, firefighters, and teachers, by restoring service levels.

DB pension plans have been job killers in recent years, and will continue to do so without reforms. For example, in 2010, Oakland police officers were given the choice to contribute 9 percent of their salary into their DB pensions and save eighty police jobs, or maintain the current agreement where police pay nothing into their pensions and see eighty jobs eliminated.[17]

The police union voted to continue paying nothing, effectively cutting eighty jobs. This decision certainly did not help the eighty police officers with less seniority who lost their jobs. Oakland City Councilman Ignacio De La Fuente lamented: "They put the interest of a few at the expense of the people who are going to be laid off. It's putting us and other cities out of business."[18] Similar decisions have cut teacher, firefighter, and other public service jobs across California, especially for younger workers trying to get started on a career path or keep their jobs.

There are important reasons, therefore, why experienced public employees, retirees, and younger public employees all should favor the reforms recommended in Chapter 8.

Benefits to Taxpayers

The objective of any public employee compensation package should be to attract the quality and quantity of labor necessary to provide essential state and local government services to the public at the lowest cost to taxpayers. Taxpayers should not overpay for government employees or government services. The pension reforms recommended in Chapter 8 would enable California governments to hire needed workers without creating pension millionaires or paying a 30-percent premium. In a state as attractive as California, which

---

17. Matthai Kuruvila, "Oakland Talks Break Down; Layoffs for 80 Cops," *San Francisco Chronicle*, July 14, 2010.

18. Kuruvila, "Oakland Talks Break Down."

is still a magnet to people from around the world, governments should not have to offer millionaire pensions to get people to work as public servants in California.

The pension changes presented in Chapter 8 would benefit taxpayers in several ways. First, freezing the DB plans and paying off unfunded liabilities over a 15 to 20 year period will save tens of billions of dollars. Rather than being a "transition cost," "freezing and amortizing" is a money saver long-term. For example, a 30-year plan to eliminate CalSTRS's unfunded liability is 35-percent less expensive than a 40-year plan.[19] Under the proposal to switch to DC plans, pension debts will be paid (which they must be assuming no partial or full repudiation), debts will stop accreting, and the debts will be paid off relatively quickly to save money and limit intergenerational redistribution of wealth.

Second, switching to DC plans shifts from the taxpayer to the employee the risks associated with variation in investment returns and future increases in longevity. Under DC plans, taxpayers are responsible only for making the initial contributions into the personal retirement accounts. They do not bear the risk of poor investment performance or longer lifespans. As a result, DC plans are always fully funded. The absence of unfunded liabilities means that general operating budgets are safe from impromptu raids to cover pension shortfalls, saving taxpayers billions in the long run or freeing money for other services.

DB plans, on the other hand, rely on investment officers appointed by pension boards to establish an investment strategy. If investment officers are wrong and markets underperform, taxpayers must pay for the mistakes. Taxpayers are the backstop and guarantors of DB plans, which encourages excessive risk-taking by pension officials—just like Fannie Mae, Freddie Mac, and

---

19. California State Teachers' Retirement System, *History of CalSTRS Funding and Presentation of Additional Scenarios,* Prepared for the Assembly Committee on Public Employees, Retirement, and Social Security, and the Senate Committee on Public Employment and Retirement, Joint Informational Hearing (West Sacramento: CalSTRS, March 2014).

taxpayer bailouts fueled reckless housing loans that produced the housing bubble during the run up to the Great Recession.

Even CalPERS has admitted that a switch to DC plans would save taxpayers billions of dollars long-term. Its assessment of Governor Schwarzenegger's 2005 proposal for such a switch calculated the 30-year savings to be upwards of $35.8 billion.[20] Similarly, the LAO estimated the savings to be as much as "several hundred million dollars to over $1 billion annually."[21] The 2005 proposal would have required all new state and local employees hired after July 1, 2007, to be enrolled in a DC plan. It also gave current employees a 6-month window to opt into the new system if they desired. As noted earlier, a complete "freeze and switch" for state employees would save at least $6 billion a year.

The long-term savings and budget transparency associated with DC plans would also improve the credit ratings of California governments, reducing borrowing costs and further saving taxpayer dollars.

Taxpayers who favor the responsible and transparent use of their tax money should support the reforms in Chapter 8.

Benefits to Voters

Taxpayers ultimately pay all the contributions into public pension plans whether the contributions come from government employers, government employees, or the jurisdiction itself (state, county, city, or school district). Because taxpayers fund the plans, voters should have the right to preapprove the initial defined-contribution rate, any increase to the rate, and any other plan details that affect pension financial obligations and funding. This is a

---

20. Testimony by CalPERS to the California State Senate Budget and Fiscal Review Subcommittee No. 4 on State Administration, General Government, Judicial, and Transportation, Budget and Fiscal Review Committee, February 15, 2005.

21. California Legislative Analyst Office, February 11, 2005.

needed check on the incentives of politicians, pension officials, government employees, and their unions to enhance pensions.

The public should have the right to know the true health of government pensions. They also should have the right to decide any pension plan details that effect current or future financial obligations, whether it is a DB or DC pension plan. Voters deserve to decide whether benefit levels are fair and affordable, or lavish and unjust.

Voters who favor open government and the public's right to provide a needed check on government power should support the reforms in Chapter 8.

Benefits to Legislators and Other Government Officials

The pension reforms recommended in Chapter 8 would promote open government, budget transparency, easier budgeting, and better recruitment of modern-era workers.

Easier Budgeting with More Transparency

Switching to DC plans would make government budgeting easier and more transparent. With DC plans, state and local governments and agency heads would be able to predict pension obligations each year since DC plans are always fully funded at a predetermined percentage of payroll.

With cost predictability, governments will know how much revenue they will need to cover their defined contributions. This cost certainty allows government officials to adopt annual budgets without the fear that skyrocketing pension costs will grab ever-larger shares of operating budgets and cut into other services.

With a DC plan, when a recession hits, falling tax revenue will make budgets tighter, yet government officials will be better able to predict and manage their pension costs and budgets than under a DB plan because contribution rates will remain constant. Contribution rates often escalate under DB plans during recessions to offset declining investment returns as stock and real-estate markets slide.

Superior Recruitment of Modern-Era Workers

DC plans can be a better recruitment tool for government employers, especially those targeting younger workers of today. The California State Personnel Board has conceded that new strategies are needed to recruit workers:

> It is incumbent upon employers today, and more specifically, every state agency and department to reconcile their workforce requirements with the personal needs and desires of current and potential employees. A number of surveys and studies have identified a shift in today's labor force from a loyalist, "hire and retire from one company" mindset to a mindset of free agency.[22]

DC plans are a better retirement vehicle for the "free agency" workers of today who stay with an employer fewer years and have more jobs during their careers. John Broadbent, Michael Palumbo, and Elizabeth Woodman have elaborated:

> More-mobile workers find DC plans relatively advantageous because benefits in these types of plans accrue more evenly through their career and are entirely portable should the worker separate from the sponsoring firm or leave the workforce for a period.[23]

A TIAA-CREF publication has also noted that DC plans provide unique benefits to younger workers:

> In a defined contribution plan, contributions made at younger ages will have a longer investment horizon, potentially growing over many years. This is true even if employees terminate service after a few years,

---

22. Archie and Ferrara, *Pension Intervention*, 35.
23. Broadbent et al., *Shift from Defined Benefit to Defined Contribution*, 20.

since accumulations continue to participate in the accounts' investment experience. In a traditional defined benefit plan, an employee's accrued benefit is generally frozen at the time he or she terminates employment. Even with moderate inflation, these benefits lose a great deal of their purchasing power by the time the employee begins retirement income.[24]

Many studies demonstrate that DC plans can give younger workers higher long-term returns.[25]

DB plans made more sense for the "hire and retire" generation of years past who were loyal to a single employer and stayed for longer tenures. A "back-loaded" DB plan with a lengthy vesting period is unattractive to modern workers. Again, John Broadbent and colleagues elaborate:

> Historically, the shift towards DC pension plans has largely been a response to changes in industrial structure and labor force composition that have given rise to an increasingly mobile workforce. DB plans, which are often not portable across employers, can penalize mobile workers since the expected pension benefit generally accrues only to employees who remain with the same employer throughout their career. DC plans avoid the accrual losses that can be associated with DB plans and provide mobile workers with much more flexible means of managing their retirement savings.[26]

With DC plans, California governments can modernize their pension systems for a twenty-first-century workforce, offering a portable pension that does not tie the fate of the pension to the fate of the government's financial

---

24. Teachers Insurance and Annuity Association–College Retirement Equities Fund (TIAA–CREF), *Pension Primer: The Hows and Whys of Replacing a Defined Benefit Plan*, "Reasons for Choosing a Defined Contribution Plan."

25. Tongxuan (Stella) Yang, *Understanding the Defined Benefit versus Defined Contribution Choice*, The Pension Research Council Working Paper, The Wharton School, University of Pennsylvania, 2005, 7.

26. Broadbent et al., *Shift from Defined Benefit to Defined Contribution*, 1.

health. These are all advantages when competing against the private sector to recruit today's best young talent.

Government officials who favor transparent budgeting and modern recruitment tools should support the reforms in Chapter 8.

10

The Moral Advantages

IN ADDITION TO the fiscal advantages, the pension reforms recommended in Chapter 8 are the right steps to take from a moral perspective. First, the proposal requires that the state government and local governments make good on pension benefits earned for work already performed. Public employees will receive all pension benefits that they have already earned.

Second, the current generation will pay most of the pension costs associated with the government services that they consumed. A 15- to 20-year amortization period prevents massive shifting of pension burdens to future generations, a feature of the reform measures that will become increasingly important as the baby-boom generation retires en masse. From 2009 through 2012, more than a quarter of California's state employees—52,000 workers—retired.[1] The pension plans need to be fully funded soon.

Third, reasonable and fully funded 401(k)–style pensions that are comparable to those offered in the private sector would not burden average citizens or future generations with more debt and taxes to create pension millionaires. As a result, government services will not be "crowded out" by staggering long-term pension costs nor will private spending or private saving be eaten up by taxes to pay for outsized pensions.

---

1. Jon Ortiz, "Why State-Employee Retirements Are On the Upswing," *Sacramento Bee*, October 9, 2014.

No longer would the public be forced to bankroll pension benefits that are unattainable for most private-sector workers. There are more working families today who are paying for public pensions that are far more flush and secure than most families could ever receive. Reasonable 401(k) pensions would establish equity and fairness.

Containing pension costs will allow governments to invest more in traditional public services such as schools, roads, libraries, maintenance, and police and fire protection, to name just a few. It is selfish and immoral for past generations to deprive future generations of the same services that they enjoyed and benefited from in order to pay overly generous pensions that past generations were unwilling to fund themselves.

Fourth, DC plans with mandatory government contributions would also ensure that current taxpayers pay the full cost of current public services, a fair and just outcome.

Finally, the approach recommended here would reduce the push for the state government to bail out local-government unfunded pension liabilities, and for the federal government to bail out California or other states of their unfunded pension liabilities. Bailouts would create huge debts for future generations that would be as immoral to impose on our children and grandchildren as the original unfunded pension liabilities themselves.

Courageous political leadership will be needed to get the reforms presented in this book adopted. Governor Brown told the *New York Times* in August 2013: "I've said there needs to be more pension reform."[2] Now is the time for change. Brown is in a position to be the elder statesman on this issue, to stand above partisanship and demonstrate true political leadership by helping to permanently solve the pension crisis. Brown and other lawmakers could leave a legacy of financial integrity for California.

If Governor Brown, the state legislature, and local politicians refuse to act, they are effectively defunding classrooms, starving social services, endanger-

---

2. Nagourney, "Brown Cheered in Second Act."

ing public safety, allowing roads and bridges to crumble, while increasing taxes and debt on our children and grandchildren. The financial assault on future generations will escalate. And future generations will be innocent victims of our fiscal failures, which is why younger generations need political leaders with the courage to protect them today.

Or perhaps that protection will have to come directly from the people with ballot initiatives. Either way, resolving California's public pension crisis is a moral imperative and essential to restoring the California dream.

Index

About the Author

LAWRENCE J. MCQUILLAN is Senior Fellow and Director of the Center on Entrepreneurial Innovation at the Independent Institute.

Dr. McQuillan's books and major studies include *California Prosperity: Roadmap to Recovery 2011, Jackpot Justice: The True Cost of America's Tort System, U.S. Tort Liability Index, The Facts about Medical Malpractice Liability Costs, U.S. Economic Freedom Index, An Empire Disaster: Why New York's Tort System Is Broken and How to Fix It, Tort Law Tally: How State Tort Reforms Affect Tort Losses and Tort Insurance Premiums,* and *Bringing More Sunshine to California: How to Expand Open Government in the Golden State.* In addition, he is the author of more than 400 articles in such leading outlets as the *Wall Street Journal, New York Times, Chicago Tribune, Los Angeles Times, San Francisco Chronicle, Investor's Business Daily, Forbes, USA Today, New York Post,* and *Encyclopaedia Britannica.*

He further created the California Golden Fleece Awards to highlight state or local spending programs or regulations that fleece California taxpayers, consumers, or businesses. He has been an advisor for the California State Assembly Judiciary Committee, Colorado Governor Bill Owens, Heritage/*Wall Street Journal* Index of Economic Freedom, Governor Arnold Schwarzenegger's task force on a constitutional spending limit for California, Law and Judiciary Policy Committee of the Georgia Chamber of Commerce, Swedish Office of Science and Technology, and others.

Dr. McQuillan has appeared on NPR, Fox Business Network, CNBC, C-SPAN, CNN, and radio stations across America.

He received his PhD in economics from George Mason University, and he has served as Chief Economist at the Illinois Policy Institute, Director of Business and Economic Studies at the Pacific Research Institute, Research Fellow at the Hoover Institution, and Founding Publisher and Contributing Editor of *Economic Issues.*

Independent Studies in Political Economy